# The Dharma Method

"An exceptional book, it is both deeply traditional and surprisingly refreshing and innovative. With an impressive command of Vedic knowledge, Chokoisky reveals the essence of dharma and confidently walks the reader through its full realization within a Western lifestyle. All this in an entertaining, uplifting, and effortlessly brilliant tone."

SHAI TUBALI, AUTHOR OF
*UNLOCKING THE 7 SECRET POWERS OF THE HEART*

"Written in an easy, conversational tone, *The Dharma Method* succeeds in breaking down a complex subject and updates ancient wisdom for the modern world. Chokoisky has written a wonderful primer for those seeking fundamental principles and practices of the spiritual path."

MARY MUELLER SHUTAN, L.AC., AUTHOR OF
*THE SPIRITUAL AWAKENING GUIDE*
AND *THE BODY DEVA*

"What a wonderful book! *The Dharma Method* explains sacred spiritual teachings in a way that's concise and digestible. It is loaded with really useful reference material and practical things you can do to reach your spiritual goal."

DARREN COCKBURN, AUTHOR OF *BEING PRESENT*

# The Dharma Method

## 7 DAILY STEPS TO SPIRITUAL ADVANCEMENT

### SIMON CHOKOISKY

Destiny Books
Rochester, Vermont

Destiny Books
One Park Street
Rochester, Vermont 05767
www.DestinyBooks.com

Text stock is SFI certified

Destiny Books is a division of Inner Traditions International

***Note to the reader:*** *This book is intended as an informational guide. The
remedies, approaches, and techniques described herein are meant to supplement,
and not to be a substitute for, professional medical care or treatment. They should
not be used to treat a serious ailment without prior consultation with a qualified
health care professional.*

**Library of Congress Cataloging-in-Publication Data**

Names: Chokoisky, Simon, author.
Title: The dharma method : 7 daily steps to spiritual advancement /
  Simon Chokoisky.
Description: Rochester, Vermont : Destiny Books, [2018] | Includes
bibliographical references and index.
Identifiers: LCCN 2018010996 | ISBN 9781620552858 (paperback) |
  ISBN 9781620552865 (ebook)
Subjects: LCSH: Spiritual life—Hinduism. | Dharma.
Classification: LCC BL1237.32 .C549 2018 | DDC 294.5/44—dc23
LC record available at https://lccn.loc.gov/2018010996

Printed and bound in the United States by Lake Book Manufacturing, Inc.
The text stock is SFI certified. The Sustainable Forestry Initiative® program
promotes sustainable forest management.

10  9  8  7  6  5  4  3  2  1

Text design and layout by Virginia Scott Bowman
This book was typeset in Garamond Premier Pro and Gill Sans with Parma Petit
and Helvetica Neue used as display typefaces.

To send correspondence to the author of this book, mail a first-class letter to the
author c/o Inner Traditions • Bear & Company, One Park Street, Rochester, VT
05767, and we will forward the communication, or contact the author directly at
**www.spirittype.com.**

ॐ श्री गुरुभ्यो नमः।

*Salutations to all the teachers who made this possible*

# Contents

# Preface and Self Test

I promise you, this book is easy to read and follow. In fact, for a long time its working title was *The Lazy Person's Guide to Enlightenment*. Unlike my previous books, which some have nicknamed "Dharma Encyclopedias," this is a short-and-sweet version of the finest spiritual teachings I've learned over the course of twenty years. Simple techniques—that work.

What may get in the way is some of the Sanskrit vocabulary— words like *dharma, sattva,* and others. But I promise (again) that this taste of the exotic will only help you better enjoy the buffet without overwhelming your palate.

The first and most obvious of these is *dharma*. I mean, it's in the title, so I probably should explain it—especially if you haven't read one of my "encyclopedias." *Dharma* means "doing the right thing." When a stranger is stuck on the side of the road, and you feel compelled to help, that's dharma. When you are working on something you love and time flies, that's also dharma. *Dharma* is perhaps best described as "rightful purpose," and the more you align yourself with it the less you suffer. In a sense, *dharma erases karma*.

Here's what I have to say about it in chapter 12 (which you can skip to right now if you want to know more):

Dharma is your inner path—the reason you were put on this planet. By following it God, love, and prosperity come closer to you. Instead of seeking them out, pursue your dharma and let them find you!

Pretty cool, right? That's why I devoted three books to it. In my first, *The Five Dharma Types: Vedic Wisdom for Discovering Your Purpose and Destiny,* I gave you the key to access your inner code—your dharma type—for personal and social fulfillment. From work and career to what type of TV, music, diet, and even what section of the armed forces works best for you, this "encyclopedia" lays out everything you need to know to find your purpose. In my next book, *Sex, Love, and Dharma,* I walked you through physical dharma for improved health and sexuality, with tons of exotic recipes, exercises, and techniques. I even showed you how to turn your home into a sanctuary instead of living in a prison of bad energy. Then, in *Gambler's Dharma,* I revealed the power of astrology for predicting the outcome of any contest—something previously thought impossible. To be able to peek over God's shoulder and witness the workings of time and space is a precious privilege, one you can learn more about in *Gambler's Dharma.*

| DHARMA LEVEL | EFFECT | BOOK |
|---|---|---|
| Social | Career, purpose, self-expression | *The Five Dharma Types* |
| Physical | Health, diet, sexuality | *Sex, Love, and Dharma* |
| Environmental | Spatial layout and physical properties of the home | *Sex, Love, and Dharma* |
| Cosmic | Astrology and karma | *Gambler's Dharma* |
| Divine | Spiritual advancement | *The Dharma Method* |

In *this* book I guide you down the final and perhaps most important path toward divine dharma by revealing eleven easy roads to enlightenment carved out for us by spiritual masters of the past. I call these shortcuts "The Dharma Method," and incorporating a few every day will put you on the fast track to enlightenment.

The last of these shortcuts, discussed in chapter 12, involves identifying your inner software—your dharma type—for which you'll need to take the test on page xi. If you already know your type, or you've read my previous books, skip directly to chapter 1 to get started. See you there!

#  DISCOVER YOUR DHARMA TYPE

For each question give ALL the answers that describe you best. For example, you can choose one, two, three, even four responses for any multiple choice question. You don't have to like the descriptions, though they should elicit a gut reaction of "Yeah, that's me!" Tally your answers and check the key at the bottom of the test. The type that receives the most points is most likely your dharma type. The one that receives the second most points likely reflects the life cycle you are in. To know more about your dharma type and current life cycle please refer to *The Five Dharma Types.*

1. **Circle the word that means the most to you or describes you best.**
   a. Freedom
   b. Loyalty
   c. Wisdom
   d. Honor
   e. Prosperity

2. **Circle the phrase that means the most to you or describes you best.**
   a. Independence and Bliss
   b. Love and Devotion
   c. Worldliness and Knowledge
   d. Discipline and Perfection
   e. Entertainment and Fun

3. **Circle the phrase that means the most to you or describes you best.**
   a. I love being alone. Sometimes I hate people, sometimes I like them, but they usually don't understand me.
   b. I don't mind being alone as long as I have something constructive and productive to do.
   c. I love being alone. I like people but I need time to spend by myself for quiet contemplation and rejuvenation.
   d. I don't mind being alone, as long as I have a goal to accomplish.
   e. I hate being alone. I prefer the company of people, even if I don't know them.

4. **Circle the phrase that means the most to you or describes you best.**

   a.  I like strange, dark, or wild and remote places no one has ever thought of or been to.

   b.  I like the plains and wide expanses of earth. I like living close to the ground, on ground floors rather than high-rise apartments.

   c.  I like high and remote places. I like upper floors, high-rise buildings, and living above others looking down.

   d.  I like challenging places, places that are high but not so high as to be remote. I like fortified and strong places.

   e.  From Beverly Hills to gently rolling slopes, I like places where the action is, places that are easy to get to but also exclusive. I like living in the middle ground, not too high, not too low, where there is activity and access to the world.

5. **Circle the sentence that describes you best.**

   a.  I am the rebel or black sheep of my family. As a parent I give freedom to my kids and let them individualize themselves from others.

   b.  I am deeply bonded with my family. As a parent I nurture my kids by making sure that they are well fed, healthy, and content.

   c.  I tend to teach my family and urge them to improve themselves. As a parent I make certain that my kids learn how to think for themselves, get a good education, and understand the world.

   d.  I am the strong one in my family. As a parent I lead by example and earn my kids' respect with discipline and order.

   e.  I actively support my family with shelter and resources. As a parent I provide for my kids and make sure that they understand the value of money, self-effort, and making your way in the world.

6. **In religion I *most* value the following:**

   a.  Going my own way.

   b.  Faith and devotion.

   c.  Study and scripture.

   d.  Penance and discipline.

   e.  Rituals and observances.

7. **In marriage I *most* value the following:**
   a. An unconventional spouse, one who understands my particular quirks and desires.
   b. A dutiful spouse who is loyal and provides for me: a woman who cooks and cleans/a man who brings home the bacon.
   c. A sensitive, intelligent spouse.
   d. A challenging spouse with whom I can do activities.
   e. A beautiful spouse.

8. **I mainly watch TV for:**
   a. Horror, alternative political and spiritual viewpoints, science fiction (like the Sci-Fi, FX, Indie, and Alternative channels).
   b. Family, drama, history, and community programs (like soap operas, reality TV, daytime shows, cartoons, entertainment gossip, and reruns).
   c. Educational, thought-provoking, human-interest stories and entertainment (like National Geographic, PBS, Sci-Fi, and documentary channels).
   d. Sports, action, news, and politics; adventure stories and entertainment (ESPN, CNN, etc.).
   e. Fun programs, drama, music, comedy, game shows, financial and motivational stories, and entertainment (like HBO, the Comedy Channel, and Spike).

9. **Under stress I tend to:**
   a. Bend the rules or lie to get my way; feel invisible and self-deprecate.
   b. Become lazy, close down in my own space, and worry a lot.
   c. Be scatterbrained, feckless, and wishy-washy.
   d. Become anger prone, inattentive, and reckless.
   e. Be moody, depressed, loud, and restless.

10. **At my best I am:**
    a. A revolutionary, an inventor, a genius.
    b. A devoted friend, a hard worker, a caregiver.
    c. A counselor, a teacher, a diplomat.
    d. A leader, a hero, a risk taker.
    e. An optimist, a self-starter, a promoter, an adventurer.

## Answer Key

Tally your answers now. The most selected letter likely reflects your dharma type.

        A. Outsider
        B. Laborer
        C. Educator
        D. Warrior
        E. Merchant

# 1
# Divinity in You

*"Yogis are lazy,"* says my mentor as we cruise by a yoga studio.

*"But they do the hardest practices—getting up early, fasting, meditating all the time . . . how can they be lazy?"* I remonstrate.

*"These are shortcuts to enlightenment. Yogis do them because they don't have time to mess with stuff that takes forever. You know, they're lazy."*

Being spiritual doesn't mean that you have to meditate in a cave eight hours a day or leave your family for a convent. It doesn't depend on brain-enhancing contraptions or the money you give to a church, because spirituality is inherent in you—it's free and easy to cultivate. The techniques in this book distill centuries of methods used by spiritual masters from around the world, including Christ, Moses, and the Buddha, who enriched their lives by investing in the dividends of an awakened inner abundance.

Like a mirror, your soul reflects the pure light of the Divine. But over time every mirror becomes dusty—caked and encrusted with the negative conditioning of material reality. Eventually, without attentive upkeep, it may become so grimy that it reflects little to no light. This is when we feel depressed, materialistic—even mean and violent. We see the mud and not the mirror. We identify with the grime, not knowing that just below it the mirror is there, ready to reflect the sun and shine if we only give it a chance.

Did you ever get a cut? What was your job to make sure it healed? Did you actually do any healing, or did you simply clean the wound and allow it to heal itself? Letting spirituality shine through you is the same—your job is to clean the junk getting in the way, letting the light do its work. That light is the reality of your true self. The only difference between "spiritual" and "material" people is how encrusted their mirrors have become, for all mirrors shine equally when they've been cleaned and polished.

It's no accident that spiritual traditions at their core teach similar truths—that love and compassion are closer to your true nature than fear and selfishness; that light triumphs over darkness; that the essential part of us is immortal, joyful, and free. "Well, that's all fine and good," you may say, "but it's not how things work in the *material* world where we have to fight to put food on the table."

It's true. In the dog-eat-dog reality of bills and daily survival, love and compassion may seem out of reach. But your spiritual nature is closer than you think and available to you 24/7 if you know how to summon it. And you don't have to be a yogi or a nun to do so. The powerful shortcuts in this book are as relevant to the seminary student as they are to the homemaker balancing work and family and will help you work *smarter,* not *harder,* to effectively clean your inner mirror. That's because they represent the best of the yoga, Christian, Buddhist, Hindu, and other traditions I have studied. As I said in the preface, this is the lazy person's guide to enlightenment, because it's about cultivating spirituality with minimum effort and maximum results.

## PURITY

In Sanskrit, one of the oldest languages in the world, the word *sattva* means "beingness"—one's essential state. This natural state is one of purity, harmony, and balance, and it's the glow you see in saints around the world. From Christ to Krishna, the halo surrounding these enlightened icons is sattva—the light of spirit suffusing the material self. Our goal is to *return* to that state by removing the grime that keeps our purity from shining through.

The Sanskrit term for this grime is *tamas,* the opposite of *sattva,* which also means "dullness, depression, and darkness." Tamas is the mud that clogs our spiritual channels and blocks our light. There are tamasic and sattvic people, places, foods, and even times of day, which we'll examine in this book. And though we'll mainly use the English equivalents of these words, it's important to know that *entire languages* have been constructed to describe the spiritual experience of moving from darkness to light (See the What's So Special about Sanskrit? box on p. 4).

It is said that the Buddha's aura of sattva was so powerful that anyone within fifty miles of him became calm and meditative. Children stopped fussing, and mothers stopped fretting. Farmers dropped their yokes to sit and contemplate. Whole villages came to inquire about the source of their calmness. In fact one of the ways to kindle your sattva is to sit in the company of those in whom it already shines brightly. Like a torch lighting others, that flame can ignite your inner spark of divinity.

That's because this halo, the *light* in *enlightenment,* doesn't belong only to saints and martyrs—*it also belongs to you.* By shedding the layers of darkness that stand in its way you can get in touch with your own personal splendor. Purity is not a finite resource like water or food, to be hoarded and saved. Though precious, it is free; though priceless, it is abundant, unburdened by the material imperatives of supply and demand—scarcity and drought. The only question is how to realize it. A master named Yeshua (Jesus) said, "My yoke is easy and my burden is light." How right he was! By practicing the principles taught in the Dharma Method *every day* you can be the source of your own enlightenment.

"What is enlightenment?"

"It is seeing things as IT IS."

"What do you mean?"

"In the dark, you mistake a rope for a snake, a lamppost for a stranger. But turn on the light, and snake and stranger disappear. Where did they go?"

"I don't know."

"They were never there in the first place. They are illusion, fabrications of the mind. So it is with most things."

"So enlightenment is seeing things as they are?"

"Enlightenment is seeing things as IT IS!"

"I still don't understand . . ."

"It's okay, it will come . . ."

### What's So Special about Sanskrit?

You may wonder why we use words like *sattva* when we could just say *purity*, *light*, and *balance*. It's not to be pretentious—it is because Sanskrit was designed to describe spiritual states perhaps more precisely than any other language on Earth. Your Volkswagen Golf may be fine for tooling around the city, but to cross the Baja Desert you need a vehicle specially equipped for that purpose. Sanskrit is the all-wheel drive truck engineered to deftly traverse the spiritual terrain, and English has already borrowed from it. The words *guru, pundit, karma, avatar, chakra, mantra,* and *yoga,* for instance, are all part of the English lexicon.

While words like *nirvana, moksha,* and *samadhi* all translate to "enlightenment," that's because we only have the word *enlightenment* in English to describe the varying nuances of the spiritual experience. *Moksha* literally means "release" and is the general term in Hinduism used to suggest release from the bonds of attachment. *Nirvana* is a Buddhist term that means "without disturbance," and *samadhi* comes from the yogic tradition meaning "complete absorption." All three describe subtle levels of awareness and together correspond to what most of us consider enlightenment.

# ENLIGHTENMENT

*Enlightenment* may mean different things to different people. It's both "the process of becoming lighter" (as opposed to carrying the heavy burden of accumulated grime) as well as being "bright and shiny" (as opposed to lurking in the dark). Both meanings are interchangeable when it comes to spirituality. Dropping the heaviness of a toxic colon, for example, by fasting or cleansing can lead one to see the world in a brighter light. However, most simply put, enlightenment means becoming "a light unto yourself." When it's dark, it's easy to mistake one thing for another, like a rope for a snake. But when the light's turned on, the snake disappears. This is seeing the truth of our existence, which is suffused with beauty, peace, and love. But don't take my word for it: here's a summary of the eleven principles that will help you experience it for yourself.

- Timing: how to choose the best times of day to charge your spiritual batteries
- Breathing: how to make your body light and your mind translucent
- Carving out time for the spirit: active and passive meditation
- Eating blessed food: the best and worst foods for cultivating purity in body and mind, when to eat them, and how to sanctify your meals
- Sacred speech: cultivating sound for a standing wave of good vibrations
- Sacred movement: turning any exercise into spiritual practice
- Honoring the elements: how to harness the purity in nature
- Fasting: how to get the most from the oldest spiritual discipline in the world
- Making your home a temple: creating space for the Divine
- Sharing good company: gods, dogs, and kids
- Doing your dharma: how to give your unique gift to the world

In the appendix you'll learn how to accrue points for doing each of these practices and how to change them up every day to suit your needs and schedule. Read the 7 of 11 section in the appendix to see how to integrate these incredibly easy and flexible methods on your path to enlightenment.

Are you ready?

Let's go!

# 2

# Rise and Shine

Whether visiting a Christian monastery or a Buddhist retreat center, one thing you'll notice is that everyone wakes up early. If you talk to successful athletes and entrepreneurs they advise the same practice, summarized in Ben Franklin's adage "Early to bed and early to rise makes a man healthy, wealthy, and wise." That's because the early morning hours are imbued with a freshness and clarity that you can only access by getting up with the sun.

Have you ever slept in? Let me rephrase—have you noticed that *when* you sleep in you wake up feeling groggy, dull, and achy and have a harder time clearing your head than when you wake up at dawn? That's because after the sun has fully risen the freshness and clarity of the morning are overwhelmed by the hustle and bustle of the day. In *Sex, Love, and Dharma: Ancient Wisdom for Modern Relationships* we described the twenty-four-hour daily cycle in depth, including what each house means, the best times for sex and exercise, and even when to ask for a raise. In this book we will look at the best times for spiritual practice, which include dawn and dusk. According to Vedic astrology each house divides the day into one of twelve slices, each with a specific meaning. The first slice, for example, has to do with the body, so it's the best time to wake up, shower, exercise, and take care of yourself. The twelfth house represents leaving home for a while, and that's when most people take off for work. The houses reflect human behavior. Make sense?

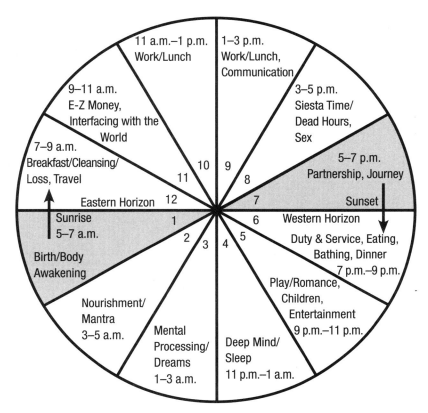

*The diurnal cycle divided into twelve parts, or houses. Each house reflects a different part of your daily biorhythm. The first and seventh houses, representing sunrise and sunset, are two of the best times for spiritual practice.*

## HERE COMES THE SUN!

Generally speaking, the hour before and after sunrise is the most tranquil part of the day. If sunrise falls at 6:00 a.m., then 5:00 to 7:00 a.m. is the ideal time to load up on the natural spiritual energies in the environment. Even if you have to take a nap later on, it's better to be up early to glean dawn's peaceful vibes. Early risers have an advantage over those who sleep in. They carry a bit of morning glory with them all day long, giving them an edge in both work and play, in their spiritual as well as material lives. Ask any millionaire or billionaire and most will tell you—the early bird gets the worm. These rules apply to everybody—

regardless of dharma type, age, race, or socioeconomic status!

Okay, now I know what you're thinking, *I thought you said this was "the lazy person's guide to enlightenment!" What if I'm not a morning person?*

If you're not an early riser don't worry. We'll explore other ways to polish your inner mirror and make it shine. Still, you should try basking in the predawn hours once in a while. Unapologetic night owls sometimes stay up until 4:00 or 5:00 a.m. to experience the incredible stillness at this time. It's one way to master the tyranny of sleep. Yogis, military personnel, and adventurers sometimes train like this, but the best way to maximize early morning purity is to be in bed early the night before.

Take the example of football great Tom Brady, whose teammates call his routine "incredibly boring." Brady comments, "I'm hopefully asleep by 9:00 o'clock. During the season, I'd say even earlier, usually 8:30 p.m., and I'm up at 5:00 or 5:30 on most mornings."[1] Not everyone has the discipline to sacrifice late-night TV and drinking with friends. But not everyone can be a Super Bowl champion either. The good news is that rising early is but one of the spiritual practices in this book, and you don't need to do them all.

Being awake at sunrise encourages the benefits of lightness, peace, and tranquillity to last into your day. Watching the sunrise—even in a reflection or through a window—takes this a step further. Exposing yourself to the rays of the rising sun is a way to charge your spiritual energy. Here's how to do it.

## ◆ DRINKING SUNSHINE

Stand barefoot (if possible) on the ground, facing the sun. Bare earth is best, but if you can't find it stand anywhere that allows you to be exposed to the rising sun's light. Let it bathe your body by exposing as much skin as practicable (just don't get arrested!). You can also double up on sunrise energy by doing a bit of yoga or t'ai chi. Try to bathe in the sunlight for ten to fifteen minutes.

Optionally you can gaze gently at the sun, imagining the sun's rays filling your body and mind with purity as you do so. Start with ten seconds at a time, building up slowly each day. This centuries-old practice is said to strengthen the eyes, brain, and heart. Be careful though—doing this beyond forty-five minutes or so after sunrise you run the risk of eye damage, especially if you're just starting out. Thus, only gaze at the sun when it is reddish or orange, within thirty to forty-five minutes after sunrise. Specifically, only practice when the UV index is below 1. You can check this online or in your local newspaper. For example, Google "UV index for Baltimore" to find what it is for Baltimore on any given day.

In Greek myth Orion the hunter regained his vision by contemplating the morning sun. This is also part of the yogic tradition of India. If you cannot see the sun rise over your eastern horizon you can try gazing at a candle flame for fifteen minutes a day, which has some of the benefits of observing the sunrise. But if your eastern exposure is totally blocked by taller buildings or other obstacles, consider moving.

Seriously. In the Vedic science of home arrangement the east and northeast are the most important directions. A home without good exposure to these suffers from a lack of the sun's positive energy, and the inhabitants of such homes may experience diminished prosperity, vitality, and spirituality. Having visual access to the sunrise underscores the realtor's cliché: "Location is everything"—more specifically, an ideal location is one that allows free and uncluttered access to the east and northeast. (There will be more on this in chapter 10.)

## HOW TO GET
## A GOOD NIGHT'S SLEEP

The greatest obstacle to rising early is poor sleep quality. It's hard to get up when your body isn't rested. This is especially true in the West where artificial light is everywhere, particularly from phone, TV, and computer screens whose light emissions are proven to disturb circadian rhythms. Add in stress from work, frequent travel, disconnect from nature (being indoors too much), and lack of exercise and we have a recipe for circadian stress. Fortunately we can manage most of these factors. Additionally, here are seven easy remedies I recommend to ensure a good night's sleep:

### *7 Hacks for Better Sleep*

- Massage the soles of your feet with coconut oil or, if they're really dry, castor oil. You can wear socks to avoid staining your sheets.
- Drop garlic oil in your ears. Lie on one side. Put half to one dropper full of garlic-mullein oil (sold in most health food stores) in your ear. You should feel like you're underwater as the oil fills the ear canal. Massage around the ear for five minutes then insert a cotton ball in your ear. Turn over and repeat for the other side. This alone puts me into dreamland. It's also superb for avoiding colds and the flu. Best to warm the bottle first by immersing it in hot water for five minutes (but never microwave or heat the oil directly).
- Put a drop or two of castor oil in your eyes before bed. Don't do this in the morning as it will blur your vision.
- Sit for fifteen minutes in passive meditation. A great segue into sleep.
- Take a zinc-magnesium supplement before bed.
- Drink a glass of warm milk spiced with nutmeg, cinnamon, cardamom, and/or ginger. You can also add a clove or two of garlic to the milk while you're warming it for a soporific effect. If you drink milk, don't supplement with zinc since the calcium will compete with zinc for absorption. Choose one or the other.
- Take melatonin. Start with a microdose of half a milligram and work your way up over the course of a few weeks. If you start to feel groggy the next morning, that may be a sign that you're taking too much. Dosages may range from .5 milligrams to 5 milligrams. Vitamin D is the "daytime" vitamin (hormone, actually), and melatonin is the nighttime hormone. In chapter 8 I go hog wild describing the effects of vitamin D and its importance to physical and spiritual health. Melatonin, it turns out, is equally important. But since I'm all out of chapters you'll have to take my word for it. Try using melatonin to see how your circadian rhythm lines up. It just might make you into a morning person after all!

*"So, why is it important to get up early?" I ask one morning.*

*"Because the devil is still sleeping."*

*"You believe in the devil?"*

*"The devil is your ego—the part of you that thinks it is separate from God; the part that believes it got where it is on its own. But nothing exists without spirit; the breath of God moves through all creation. In the morning you can still hear its whisper, before it is drowned by the din of the world."*

### *The Next Step: The Real 4:20*

If you're really dedicated you might consider rising earlier to take advantage of an even finer moment. Pot smokers wistfully refer to 4:20 (p.m.) as the ideal time to get high.* They may have a point. Late afternoon is the worst time to be up and about. That's because tamas, the opposite of sattva, prevails at this hour. This is pictured in astrology as the eighth house of the horoscope, and it presides over sex, death, and altered states of consciousness. That's why some cultures intuitively designate this period as "siesta time," preferring to spend it sleeping or even getting high rather than trying to be productive.

The real 4:20, however, is 4:20 *a.m.,* because that's when there's the most sattva (purity) in the atmosphere. Yes, I know, you're thinking: *Simon, I thought you said* sunrise *was the best?* Well, I did say that, but there are different levels of purity. The morning 4:20 is imbued with deeper sattva, and it carries a special name in Sanskrit—the *Brahma muhurta.*

*Oh Lord, there he goes with those words again!*

Okay, indulge me on this one—*Brahma muhurta* means the "moment (or hour) of Spirit." It represents the instant of creation—the conception of the day before the sunrise gives birth to it. It is the quiet peace before the twilight when everyone is still asleep, and the connection with the Divine is easiest to achieve. Think of it as heaven's internet—during the day everyone is using it, so speeds are slow and it's hard to get through. But during the Brahma muhurta, the hour of Spirit, the lines are free and you have direct access to God.

---

*The time also reflects the celebrations that take place on April 20 (4/20).

## A Spiritual Joke

*A Hindu priest is visiting the pope at the Vatican. The pope invites him into his chambers, where the priest spies a 24-karat gold phone. "What is that for?" he asks in his lilting Indian accent.*

*"Oh, that's my phone to God!" replies the pope. "It's very special, and it costs a hundred dollars a minute to use it."*

*"Oh, I see," the priest mutters, a bit perplexed.*

*After his visit he returns the favor and invites the pope to visit him in India. A year later the pope obliges and travels to the priest's humble home. There he also notices a special phone. "Is that what I think it is?" the pope asks.*

*"Yes, your holiness, that is my phone to God."*

*"Oh, wonderful," the pope exclaims, pulling out a $100 bill and handing it to the priest. "I've been meaning to talk to Him."*

*"Oh, please sir, don't worry," the priest retorts, returning the pope's offering, "from here it is a local call."*

The early 4:20 is the womb of darkness before the day is born. It is the cave where you utter your deepest, darkest secrets. It is a gap—a transition between internal and external consciousness—a supreme time to create an intention while sitting quietly in meditation or prayer.

Talk to God. Listen to God. Then get up and watch the sunrise. What a fabulous start to your day!

> The predawn time between 4:00 to 5:00 a.m. is called *Brahma muhurta* in Sanskrit—"the hour of Spirit."

This 4:20 is also the perfect time to nourish yourself. In astrology the second house rules food and sustenance. Having a light but protein-rich snack at this time is great for your body because your metabolism is primed to make the most of it without turning it into fat. Whatever calories are consumed go straight to work for you. Have a protein shake or some homemade almond milk and enjoy the energy it gives you.

Another meaning of the second house is "money." As mentioned earlier, millionaires and billionaires report that being up before the dawn is a way to get a leg up on the competition. I challenge you to get up an hour before dawn for at least forty-eight days. Spend ten to twenty minutes reciting the powerful invocation described on pages 49 and 50. Set your intention for improved prosperity and watch what happens. This simple practice alone can make the difference between a life of struggle and one of increased abundance. The only thing you have to lose is . . . sleep.

### Evening Purity

Morning's not the only time to load up on spiritual vibes. Dusk works too, but since Vedic tradition views this time as the "death of the sun" it's probably best not to gaze at the setting sun too much. Instead, use these moments to sit in meditation, facing east (not west). I know, sunsets are beautiful and this is the postcard image of a romantic evening. If you must do it, fine—just don't make it a habit. The letdown or disappointment after the sun becomes hidden behind the horizon is not good for couples nor is it great for your spiritual practice. Face east and do your active or passive meditation (see chapter 4).

Since I'm not a morning person I make up for what I miss in the dawn hours by doing my practice at sunset. There is a natural hush in nature as the waters become still and birds roost in trees (or on telephone lines) to solemnize this moment. Respect the sunset by observing this stillness in your own life. Your sattva will grow as a result!

# 3

# Breathe for Life

In the past few years yogic breathing has come out of the shadows to become a proven method for taking control of your physical, emotional, and spiritual health. Its positive effects on depression, sleep, stress, and lifestyle-related problems like diabetes and heart disease have made it into popular culture and into academia through published scientific studies.

A modern pioneer in the scientific approach is Wim Hof. He and his students proved in a laboratory setting that though injected with an endotoxin that would normally cause fever, chills, and shock, they could avoid these symptoms and consciously modulate their immune response using just their breath—something never thought possible by the scientific establishment.[1] Commenting on the study's importance, its researchers noted, "Hitherto, both the autonomic nervous system and innate immune system were regarded as systems that cannot be voluntarily influenced. The present study demonstrates that, through practicing techniques learned in a short-term training program (four to five days), the sympathetic nervous system and immune system can indeed be voluntarily influenced."[2]

## PURIFYING WITH BREATH

Yogis have long known the benefits of breathwork, some of which remain top secret even to this day. Luckily most of the effective exercises have made it into the mainstream in the twenty-first century and are now available to help us cultivate our inner light. Breathing makes you feel light, and being light is an essential step to "enlightenment." Other techniques do the same thing: fasting, getting up early, being in nature, and eating pure food all help lighten the load to lift you to new states of awareness. A pilot flying at forty thousand feet sees things someone flying at ten thousand feet can never see, not to mention someone who never leaves the ground.

Breathwork takes you higher naturally, without drugs, and its side effects are almost all positive.[3] According to Vasant Lad, eminent author and director of the Ayurvedic Institute in Albuquerque, New Mexico, the effects of yogic breathing include weight and cholesterol reduction, Alzheimer's prevention, improved red blood cell and liver function, and improved memory and mood.[4] The antidepressant effects of thirty minutes of yogic breathing every day are telling enough. The economic burden of depression in the United States is *210 billion dollars* every year.[5] Breathwork may not cure every individual, and it can even bring up health or emotional issues that make certain cases worse, but for most, the lightening effects of a breathing practice are immediate, positive, and noticeable.

### Suggested Resources

Because breathwork is best demonstrated visually or in person, here are additional resources to help you make sure that you're doing the techniques correctly.

1. You can watch me perform the exercises described in this chapter at http://spirittype.com/breathing.
2. *Pranayama for Self-Healing.* Building on the techniques in this chapter, Vasant Lad demonstrates eight additional breathing and meditation exercises essential for practitioners of yogic breathing. (If you're interested in this ancient practice, this is a great resource!)

When done right you should notice rapid improvement in mood, energy levels, and the ability to slip right into meditation with little effort. It's called *work* because it takes practice and dedication. But the results can be addictive.

---

## ◆ BREATHING TECHNIQUES

### Deep Breathing/Bellows Breath

Inhale deeply through your mouth or nose while raising your shoulders. Exhale semi-forcefully most but not all of the breath through your mouth or nose as you relax your shoulders down. Feel the tension and pressure in your body releasing as you exhale, just as you sense new life and vitality filling you on the in-breath. Repeat ten to twenty times. Do this in a relaxed manner even as you're pushing out the breath. Breathing is the most natural thing. Don't overcomplicate it by thinking too hard.

After ten to twenty breaths in this fashion, inhale one last time and let out all the air. Now hold your breath as long as is comfortable. Time yourself. The next round, try for a longer hold. When you feel the impulse to swallow, allow yourself to breathe in and enjoy a breath hold with this full inhalation in the order of ten to thirty seconds. Exhale and relax; enjoy a silent meditative state.

Repeat this two more times or go straight into the next technique.

### Belly Breathing/Skull Shining Breath

Quickly exhale, forcefully using your belly button to push the air out of your lungs. The inhale is reflexive, which will lead to another quick exhale. Repeat fifty times at first, working up to a hundred repetitions.

Over a week to ten days work up to a daily regimen of five hundred belly breaths and three rounds of deep breathing. You can alternate these or do them consecutively—it doesn't matter. You can do them before or after meditation, prayer, or exercise. Some prefer to follow the happy high they get after thirty minutes of breathing with active or passive meditation. Others like to do yoga and meditation initially and finish with yogic breathing.

If you want to be hard core, consider practicing up to a thousand belly breaths daily (this takes about fifteen to thirty minutes), or even more. At this level, yogis claim that they can lower cholesterol, improve joint function, and stave off cognitive decline. Please see your doctor before beginning even the modest practice of one hundred daily breaths. The goal, remember, is spiritual enlightenment not über fitness, though the health benefits are a welcome side effect!

Please refer to the following boxed text for a sample breathing session.

---

### Sample Breathing Session

Deep breathing: ten to thirty breaths with exhale and breath hold at the end

Belly breathing: one hundred repetitions

Deep breathing: ten to thirty breaths with exhale and breath hold at the end

Belly breathing: one hundred repetitions

Deep breathing: ten to thirty breaths with exhale and breath hold at the end

Belly breathing: one hundred to three hundred more repetitions, stopping to rest when needed

---

## A NATURAL HIGH

For many folks a drug experience is the first awakening to higher consciousness. Drugs like LSD or peyote have turned on the light for many Westerners. But in the long term, use of psychoactive substances can lead to darkness and confusion. Even natural substances like cannabinoids and psilocybin mushrooms, while great medicine, reinforce the idea that there is a normal you and a you under the influence. You become dependent on the drug for the high.

Spirituality, on the other hand, is endemic to you, independent of outside stimulus. The most abundant high is available when you dedicate yourself to natural spiritual practices. Using the breath, meditation, and periodic fasting, you'll find your mind and body teeming with spiritual euphoria that lasts instead of one that takes you to heaven only to kick you out again when the high is over. Let's take a look at one of the most powerful of these methods, meditation, in the next chapter.

# 4

# The Space Within

Meditation gets a lot of press, but what it is exactly and how it works is still a mystery to many. Some say you've got to do it twenty minutes a day. Others, that you must live your life as meditation. But what does that really *mean*? Still others prescribe complicated techniques that make you worry whether you're doing them correctly. But meditation is not another "thing" to do, it's an expression of who you are. Like all authentic spiritual practices it makes life easier by removing the barriers that keep you from being the person you came here to be.

While average Janes and Joes tend to look outside themselves for validation by watching TV or chit-chatting online, truly exceptional individuals—in business, sports or spirituality—usually find themselves by looking within. By sanctifying time for meditation you can plug in and listen to the most interesting conversationalist in the universe—God. Cleverer than any TV personality and cooler than your Facebook friends is the divine source that made you. Connecting to it is an act of defiance, a rebellion against mediocrity, a declaration of your freedom: it can make your life extraordinary. Let's take a look at two ways to do this; what I call active meditation and passive meditation.

*"Why is it so hard to meditate?"*

*"See your reflection in turbulent water. Impossible. Wait for the water to still, and your reflection appears without trying. It is so with meditation."*

# FROM A.M. TO P.M.

*A.M.* stands for *ante meridiem,* "before midday," and *P.M.* for *post meridiem,* or "after midday." But for us, *A.M.* actually means "active meditation," and *P.M.* "passive meditation." And you can do them anytime you please—morning, noon, or night.

Active meditation is any spiritual practice that requires effort or technique. This includes breathing exercises, prayer, rounds on the rosary, or even service and devotion. It includes your qigong practice as well as swimming or walking in nature, as long as these are done with focus and awareness. Yoga practice too can be active meditation . . . or it can be a contest to see who is the better acrobat in expensive tights.

> *What did you do before enlightenment?*
> *—Chop wood, carry water*
> *What do you do after enlightenment?*
> *—Chop wood, carry water*

Any activity, even chopping wood and household chores, can be active meditation when done with complete awareness. Similarly, sitting in place can be an exercise in futility if the mind is not still and focused. Let's take a look at how it's done.

## ◈ THE TECHNIQUE

For five to fifty-five minutes practice an active form of meditation, including techniques we cover in this book: deep breathing, mantra recitation, prayer, or even gentle, mindful yoga. For a specific intention use the mantra on pages 49 and 50. As you practice you can create an intention, ask a question, or otherwise "talk to God." When you're done, let it go.

Don't overdo active meditation but rather use it as a segue into passive meditation, where you simply sit and surrender your mantra, your practice, and just *be*. Sit with it for five to fifteen minutes . . . or as long as you need. Listen and let God do the talking. The answers will come. Or they won't.

I recite a mantra that takes about forty-five minutes to complete. It is an active form of meditation because you have to focus on the recital of the thousand names of the Divine. After this I either lie on the floor or continue sitting without doing anything. I just listen, watching my breath—breathing as shallowly as possible—even suspending the breath. I listen—without thinking, wanting, or even breathing—for anywhere between five minutes to forty-five minutes.

If you choose to lie down you can do *yoga nidra* (yogic sleep), which isn't really sleep at all, but passive meditation. If you drift into a restful sleep that's fine, but the goal isn't to take a nap; the goal is to be awake while your body relaxes in suspended animation.

Instead of lying on your back you can also rest on your belly in Crocodile pose, which looks like a person facedown on the floor with their forehead on their hands. Or you can go into a full prostration both as a reverence to the Divine and as a passive meditation pose. Stay in this position for as long as you like, working to go deeper into silence and witnessing awareness without thought or judgment.

Another way to segue into passive meditation is through the ritual food offering discussed in chapter 5. Presenting pure food (no meat, alcohol, or sour or pungent spices) to your altar has an effect on the brain and nervous system, as well as deep spiritual significance. It's like sitting at the table with Jesus, the prophets, or your personal deity while they eat. In India they say deities eat through the sense of smell, which is why incense, fruit, and flowers are staples of ritual food offerings.

When you're done, abide in passive meditation as the food sits on the altar, energized by your devotion. Then, when you're ready, take some to eat for yourself as an extra blessing. I can't explain how good that food tastes . . . even better than Mom's cooking!

You can choose any of the mantras or prayers from chapter 6 or create your own. The point is to carve out a chunk of time to talk to the Divine. Then, when you're done talking, listen. Just as breathing requires an inhale and exhale, enlightenment requires active and passive meditation, talking and listening.

> **Just as breathing requires an inhale and exhale, enlightenment requires active and passive meditation, talking and listening.**

## P.M. STORIES

I wrote my first book, *The Five Dharma Types,* by sitting in passive meditation, listening, and writing while the inspiration was fresh. The ideas in it are not mine so much as the transmission of divine consciousness through my limited nervous system. To this day I sometimes read it and say, "Wow! How did I think of *that*?"

In your job too you are a vehicle for divine will. Along with focused prayer or visualization (A.M.), spend some time in silence, listening—without hope, without expectation, without the dizzy din of the world spinning in your head (P.M.), and you will find your inspiration. You will have your own conversation with God and enjoy the wisdom of your inner counsel. This is the bedrock of all great achievement. You can become a person with a juggernaut idea that cannot be stopped. Let your powerful insight whisper to you, envelop you, take hold and possess you in your inner silence and you too will become unstoppable! The following is an example of the power of passive meditation.

I was worried about finances and sat to pray with the intention of breaking through the obstacles standing in the way of prosperity. After an hour reciting my favorite prayer I decided to sit and give up all thoughts, hopes, and expectations, to just abide in the energy I had generated. Slowly an idea began to arise; it grew stronger to the point of overwhelming my mind: pay attention to your wife—she needs your attention. This was so clear that I got up and went to talk to her.

That led to conversations and ultimately breakthroughs in our personal and spiritual lives. We resolved much of our financial issues through that dialogue—something we probably never would have done had I been focused only on money. By letting go and letting God, I got the signal to do exactly what I needed at exactly that moment. I can't recommend passive meditation enough!

## FIVE WAYS TO JUMP-START YOUR MEDITATION PRACTICE

If you're not the sitting-around type, below are five crutches, gimmicks, tricks, or hacks that work. I know—I said that you don't need contraptions to become enlightened, but if you already have them . . . why not use them?

1. Flotation tank: Spending time in a flotation chamber is not just for superstar athletes and movie stars. Before doing so make sure that you perform some active meditation like deep breathing for at least five minutes. You'll float even more serenely.

2. Energy work or massage: Think reiki, core synchronism, or craniosacral therapy. Shirodhara is an ayurvedic treatment wherein warm oil is streamed on your third eye for thirty minutes—deeply relaxing!

3. Cold exposure: Cold showers, diving into freezing water for a few minutes, or doing cryotherapy can clear your mind quickly and effectively, leaving you in a centered state all day long. More on this in chapter 8.

4. Zero-gravity chair with noise canceling headphones: If it's good enough for the Silicon Valley crowd, it's good enough for the rest of us.

5. Holding your breath is a real and viable way to relax the body and center the mind. Read on to see how it's done.

## ~~Don't~~ Do Hold Your Breath!

If you've ever had an MRI, you know that it can be a protracted affair. During the process a technician may ask you to hold your breath for forty seconds at a time. Depending on how many images are made, you may have to do this more than a dozen times.

Getting an MRI was my weird introduction to breath holding a few years back, and I found that during and after I felt peaceful and centered, even though the MRI machine made me feel like I was inside a coffin buried at a construction site. Forcing myself to hold my breath for as long as possible then exhaling and breathing a few extra deep breaths before holding it again allowed me to go into deep mindfulness.

Doing this later, outside of the MRI, confirmed my results. As the breath, so the mind; control the breath, you control the mind. These are not my words but the wisdom of the yogic tradition. The breath hold can be the beginning of an ever-subtler process of watching your breath until there is a natural suspension of respiration—what some call "the gap." This natural suspension is not a forced breath hold but rather what happens when you're fully engrossed in something you love or when you witness an event that "takes your breath away." These are spontaneous instances of a process you can consciously cultivate. Of course, check with your doctor before practicing any type of breath retention as this can be potentially harmful or even fatal in certain health conditions! Once you get the okay, you can practice holding your breath sitting at your altar, watching a movie, or even under water. To be effective, practice holding your breath seven to eleven times in one session, for at least thirty seconds each time.

### *TV, or Not TV?*

Some devices can help you go into meditation—others keep you from it. By far the worst of these is your TV. "The best decision I ever made was getting rid of my TV. I'm so much more at peace. I have time for meditation and hobbies, and I'm not totally stressed by the latest crisis on CNN." Statements like this from my clients are common.

Getting rid of your TV may be the easiest way to create more peace at home. If you can't do it, take mini steps by getting rid of cable, or watch only Netflix or other noncommercial programming. This may not only save you money but also your time and sanity.

Finally, minimize your online profile. Do you really need LinkedIn, Facebook, Instagram, Snapchat, and all the other time-sucking apps that keep you glued to your computer screen and hunched over your phone? Unless you're using them to find a job or boost your clientele, ditch the digital hitch and set yourself free.

### *To Trip, or Not to Trip?*

It's well known that our ancestors used drugs to find inspiration. Powerful plant substances such as ayahuasca, peyote, cannabis, and psilocybin mushrooms predate the industrial age and its chemical counterparts: DMT, mescaline, THC, LSD, ecstasy, and others.

Sometimes we get so swept up in the whirlwind of daily life that it's hard to turn off left-brain, problem-solving awareness—the inner taskmaster, the personal devil: our ego. The ego is necessary for paying bills and taking care of business in material reality. But for spiritual progress it is utterly unequipped. Like a raincoat in the desert, it only bogs you down.

To transcend the ego sometimes people turn to drugs as a way to flee the left-brain world of duties and responsibilities. Psychoactive substances can act like "ego medicine" by redirecting outward material focus toward inner spiritual reality. But like all medicine, their job is to cure illness—in this case ego overload. Medicine is supremely useful when needed, but it is only for the sick, and dependence can have its own side effects.

In the Vedic worldview all drugs are tamasic, creating dullness and heaviness in the long term, even if they lead to temporary enlightenment. It becomes easy to feel dependent on a drug to produce the spiritual state, which is ultimately disempowering. In his seminal book *Be Here Now,* Harvard-trained psychologist Ram Dass describes giving his guru Neem Karoli Baba twelve hundred micrograms of LSD—*four times* the adult dosage—with no perceptible effect. Neem Karoli Baba went about his business utterly unaffected.[1]

The Hindu god Shiva is sometimes pictured smoking ganja—marijuana—which his followers also practice, emulating their deity. However they miss an important distinction: Shiva smokes ganja not to get high but to *not* get high! He does this to illustrate that he is already higher than where the medicine can take him—to demonstrate his utter mastery of this all-powerful, consciousness-altering drug. Rare is the devotee who follows Shiva's example, because it takes tremendous self-discipline. Instead most acolytes are happy to get high but less enthusiastic about the fasting, yoga, and meditation it takes to get there on one's own.

For those who are sick with ego-fixation and a worldly mind, LSD and other drugs can be miracle medicine—analgesics that ease the pain of Newtonian existence. But only the sick need medicine. As you get yourself well you no longer need crutches to walk or drugs to make life bearable. Try the Dharma Method and see if it can help you get there naturally.

### Fire Your Lawyer

Like a lawyer, your mind's job is to protect you from trauma, manage your life, and make you comfortable. Logically it sometimes even hides things from you by storing away past hurts. But over time these past hurts and traumas pile up and create a pressure that makes life unbearable. By sitting still and allowing them to surface you can process and let them go, even though this can be uncomfortable or even painful in the short term.

Your rational mind will make excuses why you shouldn't face the pain. It will give you laundry lists of more important things to do and good arguments to distract you from your inner problems. But you are *its* boss; you can choose to look at the pain if you want to. Don't let the lawyer fool you. He cannot argue away your problems. Only you, the witness, the judge, can face the truth and set yourself free.

---

### Doing Nothing at All

*Once, at a meditation retreat where students sat for hours a day, a sweeper passed by. He laughed, saying, "You sit around all day and do nothing! You should try some real work!"*

*One of the students agreed and offered to exchange places for a day—he would take the sweeper's duties and in turn the sweeper would do everything the student did.*

*The next day at 6:00 a.m. they traded brooms for blankets and went their separate ways.*

*At 6:00 p.m. they met again, the sweeper demanding back his broom. "That's the hardest thing I've ever done!" he told the student. "I'll take my broom, thank you!"*

---

Have you ever sat in a class feeling anxious or bored, your mind giving you good reasons to get up and leave? *It is not the right subject* or *The teacher doesn't like me,* you may think. Instead of listening, however, try sitting with the anxiety. Where is it coming from? Where in your body is it expressing? Maybe it's heartburn—a result of bad diet and poor digestion. Maybe you have stored anger that wants to come out. Watch the anger—or any emotion that arises—without judgment. Let it come up. Sense what body parts it moves through and how it makes you feel. Make it a point to exercise that part of your body the next time you do yoga or go to the gym. Make it a point to go to the chiropractor or get a massage or simply stretch the areas that hurt. A deeper part of yourself waits for the moments when you are still. A deeper part of yourself arises when you let it. Witnessing and watching is not being idle but active—a direct way to release pain in your body and mind. It takes a hero to do it: stillness takes work.

> Witnessing and watching is not being idle but active—a direct way to release pain in your body and mind. It takes a hero to do it: stillness takes work.

## HEAR THE MIND OF GOD

Sit every day in passive meditation and let your body and mind talk to you. Witness what they have to say. And when they become silent, listen to the mind of God. Perhaps the most important reason to witness your body and mind is to allow them to grow still, which leaves you with the universal hum, the sound of divinity. This is the real meaning of "Be still and know that I am God."

The definition of *yoga* is "ceasing the fluctuations of the mind/body stuff." With active meditation you encourage the stuff to come out; in passive meditation you witness it go and invite stillness in its stead.

*"What is yoga?"*

*"Sit still for three hours and don't move. That is yoga."*

*"My legs fall asleep when I sit for more than thirty minutes. What should I do?"*

*"Forget legs. Let them go numb. Forget everything and sit without moving. You will know yoga."*

No matter how bad my day has been, no matter how poorly I've eaten or how many hours after sunrise I finally get up . . . sunset meditation is my salvation. It is my penance and absolution. It is my stairway to sattva. I would not trade the forty-five minutes on my blanket for any drug or contraption. I would not trade it for another man's enlightenment. It is the slice of heaven I've earned with the meager power of my austerity. Talking to God and then listening, done for forty-eight days, either at sunrise or sunset, will change your life. Guaranteed, or your money back.

---

### The Best Times for Prayer and Meditation

The real 4:20, as discussed in chapter 2, is the time before sunrise when there is a hush over the land and most folks rest in silent slumber. This is called the hour of Spirit, when the human-God connection is easiest to make. Though this practice takes dedication, the early predawn hours are preferred by hard-core spiritual gangsters.

**Sunrise.** Sunrise is a juncture between night and day, and junctures in space and time are auspicious for spiritual contemplation. (Such junctures however, like eclipses, are decidedly *not* auspicious for mundane activities like marriage or starting a business.) Sattva is abundant at sunrise, and breathwork as well as moving meditations like yoga or qigong are particularly powerful. Sun gazing is another practice that has great merit, but only at sunrise.

**Sunset.** Sunset is another juncture, and while too much sun gazing at this time is not recommended in the Vedic tradition as it represents the *death* of the sun, spiritual practice is. Sit facing east and meditate. This is my favorite time—probably because I'm too lazy in the morning but also because it completes the day, and the stillness of this juncture allows me to settle down and "listen" to what nature has to say.

**"The Fifth House."** Look at the illustration on page 7. The fifth house in the daily cycle is the time between around one-and-a-half hours to three hours after sunset, though this can change by a half hour or so depending on the time of year and your location. You should be able to *feel* the fifth house, which sets in as a need for fun, play, and entertainment. Besides watching TV or going to the movies, worship, prayer, and ritual are also highly effective now. The relaxed energy you get after eating a nice dinner and settling in for the evening translates into divine worship very well. See my book *Sex, Love, and Dharma* for more juicy secrets about this period, which is also optimal for sex and making babies.

**One's birth time.** You can experiment with sitting for prayer or meditation at the time of your birth. If you were born at 2:00 p.m. try sitting at 2:00 p.m. every day to see if it connects you to the Divine. This practice works for some, because it represents a symbolic juncture—the time you came onto this planet. If you were born in the dead of night, this may be difficult to pull off, but who knows, you might like being up at your personal witching hour!

## MERGING ACTIVE AND PASSIVE

At some point you'll notice that even when you're actively practicing— say, chanting a mantra or doing breathwork—active meditation melts into passive awareness, and the mantra begins chanting itself. The doer disappears and only the action of doing remains. The way to slip from active to passive meditation is to surrender every practice to the Divine—to give the fruits of your spiritual work to your higher self or your personal deity, which we'll explore below. Then your actions become free of agenda and attachment, and you move from worship to absorption, one practice at a time.

*Thoughts come and go like passing clouds.*
*Treat them as uninvited guests*
*and continue to witness*
*the movement of your mind.*
*Behind the movement of thought*
*exists your pure Self—Asmita—*
*you know it as the feeling, "I am" or "I exist."*
*Become one with this witnessing awareness*
*and jump into the inner abyss . . .*
*Dive into this inner space*
*And discover who you really are*
*What is your original face?*

ExCERPTED FROM "THE WITNESS," A POEM BY
VASANT LAD, FROM *STRANDS OF ETERNITY*

# THE DIVINE SECRETARY

Letting go and letting God is easy if you have an emissary, a go-between, a personal deity to link you to the absolute. This personal deity (called *ishta devata* in Sanskrit) is like the Big Boss's secretary: to get to him, you must go through his secretary first. The secretary is the Boss's public face, and he or she sets all the appointments. Becoming friendly with them gets you "insider" access to the Boss. This is a silly example, but the point is that every family has a *familial deity*—usually linked to the religion practiced in that household. Every individual also has a *personal deity*—a customized image of God that makes the most sense to them.

Is it Jesus with blue eyes and light-brown hair or a swarthier, more mysterious form of the Lamb of God? Is it Mother Mary or one of the various saints? Is it Goddess or God? Or neither? If you don't know who your personal deity is, it can be found in your horoscope. Or if you have access to enlightened teachers, why not use them to help you find it? One of the greatest perks of hanging around enlightened people is that their divinity rubs off on you, a topic we discuss in chapter 11. If you don't have access to a capable astrologer or an authentic spiritual master you can meditate on the form of God that comes to you most often or that feels most comfortable.

## *The Hindu Trinity*

In Hinduism there are many gods to choose from. This is to accommodate the various ways in which people interface with the Divine. The most common "secretaries," or faces, of the absolute are represented in the following three primary forms, each of which has a male (Brahma, Vishnu, Shiva) and female (Sarasvati, Lakshmi, and Kali) aspect.

**Brahma** is the creative force of nature, but for complicated reasons he is rarely worshipped. Only a handful of temples in all of India are dedicated to him, while the other five faces of the Divine enjoy widespread worship. **Sarasvati** is the feminine counterpart to Brahma and the cultural and creative aspect of the Divine Feminine, bringing art, knowledge, and wisdom to humankind. Sarasvati is worshipped by persons who want to do better in school; excel in music, art, and language; and gain spiritual knowledge and wisdom. Sarasvati encourages purity through creativity.

**Vishnu** is the preserving force. He is also the form of God most worshipped in India, in the visage of one of his ten avatars, or earthly incarnations. Meditations on Vishnu or one of his incarnations (such as Rama or Krishna) are good for householders and those who seek financial, physical, and familial security. Vishnu is also prescribed for anyone doing counseling work, as meditation on him helps purify our inner mirror so others can see themselves in it too. **Lakshmi,** Vishnu's feminine counterpart, brings abundance and prosperity in the form of wealth, health, family, and security. It is one thing to have money and quite another to be truly fulfilled by all the abundance in your life and share it with the world. Lakshmi helps you do just that.

**Shiva** represents the destructive force in nature. Meditations on this force of divinity as represented by Shiva, and his counterpart, **Kali,** is good for those who want to break through personal problems, overcome severe health or other barriers, or those who work in "fierce" professions such as the military. Shiva and Kali encourage sattva by targeting and destroying tamas. They are good for practitioners who have a little extra "dark" side! Kali rips away illusion, bringing direct spiritual awakening and insight. She also champions underdogs and sees all races, creeds, and castes equally.

These are some of the ways to interface with the divine. Ultimately God is everywhere, and in the next chapter we will look at how to take our spirituality off the meditation mat and into our daily life by making it part of our most important ritual—eating. For more information on how to track your meditation progress, please refer to the appendix.

# 5

# Sacred Food

In this chapter we'll examine how some foods support your spiritual light while others make it harder to see. For example, according to Eastern traditions, while onions and garlic may promote physical vitality they're not so good for your spiritual health because they promote passion, agitation, and an unbalanced mind whereas foods like fresh fruits and vegetables purify the mind.

Certain foods are inherently cleaner than others. In fact, like everything else in nature, food can be classed into three categories:

*sattvic* (enlightening)
*rajasic* (stimulating)
*tamasic* (dulling)

The table on pages 33–34 lists foods for each of these three categories as noted by our ancient sages thousands of years ago.

Through careful observation and trial and error we too can experience enlightening foods bringing joy to our minds and lightness to our bodies. We can also observe how eating primarily stimulating foods like sugar, chocolate, and caffeine makes us energetic in the short term but also prone to moodiness, attachment, and inflammation. Finally, we can witness how dulling foods like Spam or fried meat make us blunt, violent, and self-destructive.

# ENLIGHTENING, STIMULATING, AND DULLING FOODS

| ENLIGHTENING FOODS (SATTVIC) | STIMULATING FOODS (RAJASIC) | DULLING FOODS (TAMASIC) |
|---|---|---|
| **Dairy:** Organic, grass-fed, non-homogenized, home-raised cow or goat milk, ghee, fresh homemade soft cheese, homemade yogurt | **Dairy:** Sour cream, salted butter, cream, cottage cheese, ice cream | **Dairy:** Hard cheeses, aged cheeses (bleu), processed milk, eggs |
| **Fruits:** Most fruits in general, including mango, pomegranate, coconut, figs, dates, peaches, pears | **Fruits:** Sour fruits including most citrus, tamarind, banana, apples | **Fruit:** Avocado, durian, watermelon, plums, apricots‡ |
| **Vegetables:** Most, including sweet potato, sprouts, leafy greens, zucchini, yellow squash, asparagus; avoid pungent vegetables and fungi | **Vegetables:** Potatoes, nightshades,† cauliflower, broccoli, spinach, winter squash, pickles | **Vegetables:** Mushrooms, garlic, onion, pumpkin, scallion, leek, chives |
| **Grains:** Basmati rice, quinoa, blue corn, tapioca, barley, spelt, oats, sprouted grains | **Grains:** Millet, corn, buckwheat, white (processed) bread (also dulling) | **Grains:** Conventional wheat, yeasty bread, brown rice |
| **Legumes:** Mung beans, bean sprouts, red and yellow lentils, chickpeas* | **Nuts and Seeds:** Brown sesame seeds, most nuts, especially if heavily roasted and salted | **Nuts and Seeds:** Peanuts, black sesame seeds, overly processed or rancid nuts |
| **Nuts and Seeds:** Almonds (especially soaked and peeled), white sesame seeds, fresh cashews | **Sauces & Spices:** Ketchup; most sour, tangy sauces, including curry and chili; cayenne, black pepper, clove | **Spices:** Jalapeño, nutmeg |
| | **Sweets:** Processed sugar, cooked honey, artificial sweeteners (also dulling) | **Sweets:** Molasses, soft drinks, stevia, artificial sweeteners, extremely sweet-tasting foods |

*Most grains and legumes tend to be enlightening; as with other foods, how they are prepared and spiced makes the difference. Sprouted beans tend to be more enlightening.

†Some experts consider nightshades dulling while others say they are stimulating. As with grains, much depends upon how they are prepared. If well-cooked and spiced they can be stimulating. If not, they become more difficult to digest, hence dulling. Leftover food, no matter how enlightening to begin with, becomes dulling as bacteria take over.

‡Most fruit is enlightening. Those fruits in the *stimulating* and *dulling* columns are *relatively* less enlightening than the fruits in the first column. Watermelon, for example, is not as dulling as, say, fried pork.

## ENLIGHTENING, STIMULATING, AND DULLING FOODS (continued)

| ENLIGHTENING FOODS (SATTVIC) | STIMULATING FOODS (RAJASIC) | DULLING FOODS (TAMASIC) |
|---|---|---|
| **Spices:** Saffron, turmeric, cardamom, coriander, fennel, cumin, ginger | **Meats:** Chicken, fish, most seafood | **Meat:** Most, including beef, pork, lamb, venison |
| **Sweets:** Fresh sugarcane juice, raw sugar and honey | **Sour, salty, pungent foods:** Pickles, vinegar, wine (also dulling) | **Beverages:** Alcohol, soft drinks, energy drinks |
| **Meats:** None | **Caffeinated foods:** Chocolate | **Stale food, leftovers** |
| **Beverages:** Licorice and other teas | **Beverages:** Coffee, black and green tea, soda (also dulling), energy drinks (also dulling) | **Most drugs** |

> Leftover food, no matter how enlightening to begin with, becomes dulling as bacteria take over.

Science is catching up to the wisdom of the ancients. Current studies with titles like "Evolution of Well-Being and Happiness after Increases in Consumption of Fruit and Vegetables" and "Let Them Eat Fruit! The Effect of Fruit and Vegetable Consumption on Psychological Well-Being in Young Adults" conclude that people who (sometimes force themselves to) consume more fresh fruits and vegetables are happier, have more stable moods, and live longer.[1] The results from one study that collected data from more than twelve thousand participants noted: "Increased fruit and vegetable consumption was predictive of increased happiness, life satisfaction, and well-being . . . equal in size to the psychological gain of moving from unemployment to employment. Improvements occurred within 24 months."[2]

The verdict? Eating fruits and vegetables cleans your inner mirror and promotes enlightenment. You can feel it every day by eating from the *enlightening* food list above.

"Increased fruit and vegetable consumption was predictive
of increased happiness, life satisfaction, and well-being . . .
equal in size to the psychological gain of moving
from unemployment to employment."

## Q&A ABOUT FOOD CHOICES

*I thought garlic and onions were good for you! They're vegetables too. Why aren't they enlightening?*

Generally, eating fruits and vegetables regularly will make you a happier person, but not all vegetables are created equally. For example, mushrooms, garlic, onions, and nightshades like potatoes and tomatoes disturb the body and mind in various ways by creating passion, digestive problems, or introducing lectins and toxins that are difficult to process. A food can be good for you physically—like garlic or certain mushrooms. But that doesn't mean it is necessarily good for you spiritually. Mushrooms are a fungus—an animal life-form with its own consciousness that can dull or even take over the human mind. But mushrooms can also be highly beneficial in small quantities. From kefir to kombucha, and cordyceps to psilocybin, mushrooms can benefit human health when used medicinally and with respect. But the caveat remains—even psychoactive mushrooms, which may promote enlightenment in the short term, come with side effects and a long-term dulling consequence on the mind. These fall under the category of "medicine," as discussed in chapter 4. Garlic, on the other hand, engenders sex drive and passion, but this can also lead to problems, steering the mind and heart from love toward lust. Garlic is therefore avoided by spiritual practitioners who wish to become more subtle and light rather than gross and animalistic.

A food can be good for you physically . . .
but not necessarily spiritually.

*What about dairy? Why is milk enlightening? Isn't it hard to digest?*

We should define what we mean here, because the beverage we

drink today is not what the ancients thought of as milk. To be precise, the list should read "pasture-raised, organic, non-homogenized, small-batch, happy-cow produced milk." Part of the reason modern folks cannot digest dairy is because corporate farming practices ensure that it's nearly impossible to obtain pure milk.

The beverage we drink is homogenized and contains hormones and antibiotics. Because it is also forcefully milked, the cow doesn't pass down sweet thoughts to you, only anxiety and sadness. Just as a mother transfers love and immunity to her baby, so a cow can confer those qualities to whomever drinks her milk, provided she is well taken care of. For these reasons it's perhaps best to minimize dairy on the All-Saints Diet described later in this chapter. Even if you choose to have dairy, make sure you avoid hard cheeses. Fresh homemade cheese and yogurt are enlightening; store-bought stuff is not.

How we drink milk is also a problem. According to ayurveda, milk is supposed to be kept raw until it is ready to drink, then boiled with spices like ginger, turmeric, cardamom, and cinnamon and allowed to cool before drinking. Never drink milk straight from the fridge. Cold milk is mucus-forming and harder to digest than warmed, spiced milk. Homogenization is also difficult on the body. In regular milk, fat and protein molecules vary in size, making it easier for your gut to differentiate between them. Homogenized milk squeezes the fat molecules, making them smaller and harder for the body to recognize. This "dumbing down" of the cellular intelligence leads to clogging of the inner pathways and more toxins in the body.

### What about meat and fish?

Even though they're not enlightening, meat and fish once in a while are not deal breakers, especially when eaten seasonally. John Douillard, in his book *The 3 Season Diet,* explains how our bodies have evolved different digestion strategies for each of the three seasons—winter, spring, and summer. Eating heavy foods like meat during the cold winter months helps us to survive and thrive. Carrying this diet into the spring and summer, however, can spell disaster. That's why nature tends to give us what we need for every season: meat and root vegetables in the winter, berries and greens in the spring, and fruits and grain in the summer. If you live in a tropical climate without a real winter it is easier to follow a pure vegan, vegetarian, or All-Saints Diet. If, however, you live in a more northerly clime such as Alaska, meat and fish may be closer to a year-round staple and make a pure All-Saints Diet harder to follow.

***What about sugar? You say sugar isn't enlightening, but don't fruits and starches have sugar . . . What gives?***

Processed sugar is stimulating whereas naturally occurring sugars are enlightening. That includes the sugar in starches like basmati rice, spelt, and other grains. Among sweeteners, maple syrup and raw honey are relatively pure, even though honey is plundered from bees and maple syrup from trees. Other sweeteners like white sugar and high-fructose corn syrup are worse. Stick with a good, local, raw honey and you'll gain the bonus benefits of allergy protection and fat mobilization, especially during the spring allergy season.* According to ayurveda, honey is "scraping" and "warming," and when not used in excess (under two tablespoons a day) it can be an effective way to cleanse your body while helping to control weight and fortify immunity.

Fruit should be eaten alone. Eating fruit by itself is enlightening; eating it with dairy, meat, wheat, or pretty much anything else is not. Part of the reason is because fruit digests more quickly than other foods. When mixed with other foods, the fruit cannot pass through at its usual rate and so ferments in the GI tract, causing morbid mucoid plaque and toxicity in your system. Spare yourself these problems by following ayurvedic protocol: eat fruit by itself, and enjoy the enlightening benefits proposed by the ancients and proved by modern science.

Fitness and nutrition expert Jack LaLane used to say that he only shopped from the outside perimeter of a store where the fresh fruit and vegetables, dairy, meat, and fish were. Everything in the middle is the

---

*Adding local bee pollen to your raw honey is a great way to combat seasonal allergies.

packaged stuff he avoided. He was bright and energetic well into his nineties. You can be too if you follow his advice.

## THE ALL-SAINTS DIET

The bible recounts how Daniel fasted for three weeks in order to understand a vision from God. This "Daniel Fast" is now practiced by some Christians, and involves eating only fruits, vegetables, and whole grains while drinking only pure water. This is basically an enlightening-food program, what I term the All-Saints Diet (since most saints followed it).

I challenge you to try eating enlightening food for a month. You will see a dramatic change in your thinking. You will feel motivated, light, and spiritually awakened. In India gurus sometimes put their students on a milk-only fast for forty days to prepare them for spiritual study. This, in addition to sitting in an unfurnished room for the duration of that period, ensures that they develop a clear mind and learn to sit quietly without distractions, cushions, or accessories.

You don't have to go to such extremes, and a milk-only diet in America would likely be a disaster, since it's nearly impossible to find organic, happy cows to milk for daily sustenance. Before the nineteenth century, in India as elsewhere, refrigerators didn't exist, and dairy had to be milked fresh and drunk quickly or preserved as butter, yogurt, or cheese.

But for the All-Saints Diet you can eat any of the foods in the *enlightening* column in the table at the start of this chapter (see pages 33–34). Simply follow these guidelines.

---

### The All-Saints Food Checklist

In most cases . . .
- If it's canned or in a wrapper it's not enlightening.
- If it's leftover from yesterday, it's not enlightening.
- If it's made from animals, it's not enlightening.
- Eat fruit alone.
- Never cook with honey.

---

- Never cook with honey. Raw honey is nectar. Cooked honey is poison. It is okay to put a teaspoon of honey into your tea *after* it has steeped, but not before. That's because warm tea is not enough to degrade the honey, but boiling or baking with it is. Look for "Raw" and "Unfiltered" on the label and avoid "Honey Blends" or "Honey Products."*

- Again, eat fruit alone or, if you must, with nuts or seeds. Especially avoid mixing fruit with meat or dairy as this is a toxic combination. It is best to eat fruit by itself.

- Avoid "dead" foods as much as possible, which include meat and canned, wrapped, preserved, and fermented products. Though they may be "good" for you, fermented products contain concentrated animal life—bacteria—that doesn't contribute to an enlightened mind, except in small helpings. For that reason only fresh homemade yogurt makes it to the enlightened food list.

- Avoid exposure to chemicals and pollution in your environment. Cigarettes, coffee, and alcohol are out, as is tap water, which is usually fluoridated. Opt for pure spring or even distilled water on your All-Saints Diet.

- During winter you can cook wholesome soups and porridges. If it is summer or spring, try eating mainly uncooked (raw) berries, fruits, and vegetables. There are countless recipes to be found in good ayurvedic cookbooks on the subject.[3]

### Additional Tips
Here are a few more pointers for stoking your digestive fire and turning on the inner light.

- Eat only when you're hungry.
- When you eat, do not fill your belly to more than 75 percent full.

---

*Filtered honey contains zero pollen—the allergy-fighting component present in the raw, unfiltered stuff. Also make sure that you source your supply from local beekeepers or buy New Zealand Manuka honey, because it's easy for cheap, ultra-filtered Chinese honey to make it to your table and into your body if you're not careful. Foreign and cheaply made honey often has by-products like antibiotics and heavy metals, and sometimes even comes with a "Made in the USA" sticker. As with milk, so with honey—buyer beware!

Like your washing machine, you want to leave a little room for your stomach to efficiently do its work.

- As much as is practical, eat foods that are in season where you live.
- Eat no more than three times a day, giving your body time to digest.
- Avoid very sour, salty, pungent, or bitter foods and spices as these are dulling.
- In addition to minimizing tobacco and alcohol, completely avoid cannabis and other drugs as they are dulling.
- Eat your water and drink your food, which means you should chew solid food so well that it turns liquid in your mouth. Also swish and "chew" your water instead of just gulping it down so it mixes with your saliva and becomes easily assimilated in the body. Gulping down food or water is a bad idea with respect to both digestion and spiritual awareness.

Sometimes you won't have access to pure, organic food, or it is too expensive, or you just don't have time to cook enlightening meals. Or maybe you like to eat meat. Don't fret. There are other ways to purify your meals, specifically through ritual, awareness, and blessing.

## BRING AWARENESS TO YOUR FOOD

Creating a ritual is a first step to making mealtime more meaningful. This entails taking a moment before eating to say grace, light a candle, or otherwise bless your food. A Harvard study showed that participants who performed a brief ritual before eating found their meal tastier, more satisfying, and of higher quality than those who didn't.[4] Chanting a mantra or prayer before eating is a way to bless even the humblest meal, inviting grace into your life.

More important than the purity of your food is the purity of awareness you bring to it. Awareness is focused by the breath; the breath is focused by sound; sound is focused by language, and the essence of language is mantra or prayer. Reciting a mantra or prayer as you cook or eat will translate consciousness into vibration, intention into action, and food into nectar. Refer to the following chapter for specific prayers.

Reciting a mantra or prayer as you cook or eat will translate consciousness into vibration, intention into action, and food into nectar.

Here are some ways to ritualize your meals.

- Say a mantra or prayer from your spiritual tradition.
- Light a candle and set the table in a way that creates sacred space. The candle represents your inner digestive fire and the flame of awareness.
- Create a separate space for eating aside from your home office, TV area, or bedroom. Eating is its own business. Don't mix it with other activities.
- Cut TV and other distractions while eating, including too much talking. When your focus is on the TV or a heated conversation, your digestion suffers. What's more, studies show you will likely overeat. For the sake of your waistline, if nothing else, eat simply and without distractions.

## Mindful Eating

Eating deliberately feeds into the next step, which is taking time to eat your food. When you eat without hurry, your body has an easier time recognizing and assimilating the food you give it. This recognition helps digestion and creates a smoother transit through your system. Even enlightening food turns dull when eaten in a hurry. The freshest fruit and salads, not to mention fast food, become toxic when they're not eaten properly. Take your time and enjoy your meals. This extends to preparing, cooking, setting the table, and eating together as a family. If you're so busy that you don't have time for this, consider intermittent fasting as discussed in chapter 9. Intermittent fasting frees up much of your day so you can sit and enjoy your evening meal in luxury.

Even enlightening food turns dull when eaten in a hurry.

Food brings people together; it is a social glue of sorts. Consuming fast food and eating in a hurry downplay the role of ritual and family bonding. As a result people grow disconnected from their families and from the health and satisfaction derived from eating. Studies show that kids and teenagers of families who eat together regularly do better in school, are less likely to use drugs and rebel, and are healthier overall. Give your food more time, and your food will give you more life![5]

> Give your food more time, and your food
> will give you more life!

### *Sanctify Your Food*

Even organically grown, enlightening food prepared without love cannot compare to ordinary fare prepared by someone who loves you. After all, there's no cooking like Mom's cooking, even if Mom doesn't use the purest ingredients. If Mom's blessing is good, God's blessing is even better. Eating blessed food means taking time to offer it to the Divine well before you put it in your mouth. In Sanskrit this is called *prasada*—divine leftover (the only kind of leftovers allowed on the All-Saints Diet).

*Prasada* (also written *prasad* in modern Hindi) means "serenity," "blessing," and "clarity" and refers to the settled feeling of grace and blessedness one feels after eating food that has been offered to the Divine. Prasad is not just the cracker you eat in church on Sundays—it is the everyday offering at your own personal altar that you can enjoy as divine leftovers.

Never offer dulling food like meat, eggs, or garlic unless specifically guided to do so. That means even cookies made with eggs are out. Fresh, naturally sweet food like fruit and whole grains are best. Nuts and dairy also fit the bill. Simple rice pudding is a perennial favorite. Despite being sweetened with sugar, it is considered an enlightening treat overall.

Following is a guide on how to sanctify your food.

## ◆ OFFERING FOOD TO THE DIVINE

Every morning (or when you feel inspired) present a plate of enlightening food on your altar.

Along with your food presentation light a candle and offer some incense and perhaps a cup of water. You may also sprinkle water on your food offering as you say a prayer.

An example of a prayer in English is "Oh Lord! I offer these fruits and their life-supporting force for your enjoyment. I also offer this light, incense, and water. Please accept my offering, however humble it may be. Amen." Such invocations may range from simple to utterly elaborate.

After your invocation and/or meditation you can partake of the offering or leave the room and proceed with your day. When you are ready to enjoy the prasad, eat it alone, add it to a meal, or share it with others. A little goes a long way, and only a bite is sufficient to get the full effect. Eating blessed food carries spiritual benefits above and beyond an organic or even enlightening food diet. Repeat every day for blessings to accrue!

## RETURNING WHAT IS NOT YOURS

Sometimes eating enlightening food is not enough. Sometimes it's hard to break long-standing addictions to coffee, cigarettes, alcohol, and other "medicines" we use to get through the day. Perhaps you're looking for a way to cut your connection to short-term fixes that have long-term health detriments, such as fried foods and sweets. You might be surprised that these addictions may not even be yours in the first place! Have you ended a relationship with a partner or place of employment and are looking to rid yourself of the negativity they created in your life? Offering back what's not yours can free you from the bonds of dependence that hold you down. Let's see how it's done.

### Appease Your Ancestors . . . with Donuts?

So many of our thoughts and desires are inherited from our ancestors—both by nature and nurture—through our genetics and how we were raised. When a person doesn't fulfill their hopes and dreams in this life they may pass these desires on to their children. That is why many of the issues we think are ours actually come from our parents, who consciously or unconsciously put them into us. Have a devilish devotion to donuts? Or a rapacious relish for rum? It may not be just your sugar lust speaking but rather that of your forebears. One way to deal with these addictions is to offer them back. Give back what you crave to your ancestors so you stop craving it.

Give back what you crave to your ancestors so you stop craving it.

You can do this every Saturday or on the new moon. You can also perform a yearly offering on the day that particular relative died. In India in the fall there is a special period devoted to the ancestors called Pitri Paksha. This ancestral fortnight* begins on a full moon and ends on the new moon day consecrated specially to the dead. Other cultures have similar traditions including Dia de los Muertos and All Hallows' Eve. Fall and winter represent death and dying, when it's a good time to remember those who have come before us.

## ANCESTOR HONORING (PITRI PAKSHA)
### Dates for Delhi, India

| YEAR | DATE RANGE | NEW MOON DAY |
|---|---|---|
| 2018 | September 24 – October 8 | October 8 |
| 2019 | September 13 – September 28 | September 28 |
| 2020 | September 1 – September 17 | September 17 |
| 2021 | September 20 – October 6 | October 6 |
| 2022 | September 10 – September 25 | September 25 |
| 2023 | September 29 – October 14 | October 14 |
| 2024 | September 17 – October 2 | October 2 |
| 2025 | September 7 – September 21 | September 21 |

---

*A fortnight is a period of fourteen days, and Pitri Paksha happens during the waning, or dark fortnight, that usually falls in September. (To find the exact dates of the year for your given location, visit www.drikpanchang.com/vrats/shraddhadates.html.)

## ANCESTOR HONORING (PITRI PAKSHA)
### Dates for Phoenix, Arizona

| YEAR | DATE RANGE | NEW MOON DAY |
|------|-----------|--------------|
| 2018 | September 24 – October 8 | October 8 |
| 2019 | September 13 – September 27 | September 27 |
| 2020 | September 1 – September 16 | September 16 |
| 2021 | September 20 – October 5 | October 5 |
| 2022 | September 9 – September 25 | September 25 |
| 2023 | September 28 – October 13 | October 13 |
| 2024 | September 17 – October 1 | October 1 |
| 2025 | September 6 – September 20 | September 20 |

The new moon day of the ancestral fortnight is the most powerful day of the year for offering back to our ancestors the objects of their desire. Was Grandpa a smoker? Light him a cigarette. Did Aunt Sally have a hankering for beer and pretzels? . . . Well, you get the picture. Whether you do this weekly, monthly, or once a year, following are some suggestions.

## ◇ HONORING THE DEAD

Among your offerings include a candle, a glass of water, and your ancestor's preferred foods. Include tobacco or alcohol if these were part of their habits. Usually sweets are best, as we want to "sweeten" our relationship with the departed.

Say a prayer and offer these items back to them. Ask if they need anything from you. Set your intention as you offer these foods so that you also release any negative attachments to them yourself. After food is offered to the dead, *never* eat it. It should be discarded in nature, left to animals, or thrown in a river.

### Burning Attachments

In addition to honoring your ancestors Vedic traditions prescribe fire ceremonies for cutting ties to old habits, making oblations to the fire by saying, "This is not mine"—*idam na mama* (pronouced as "eedum nuh muh muh"). Those serious about kindling their power and taking control of their lives perform such a ceremony twice a day (at dawn and again at dusk).

This requires discipline and a rigid schedule—being tied to sunrise and sunset every day—as well as having plenty of the necessary accoutrements on hand, such as dried cow dung and ghee to keep the fire going. If this isn't feasible but you'd still like to try the fire ceremony, you can modify its setup. The spirit of the ritual is what's important.

The essence is to release what's not yours into the fire, burning it up forever. Normally when we make behavioral changes we trade one vice for another, repressing one addiction while creating a new one. We stop drinking, but become addicted to cigarettes or coffee. Or, by suppressing our anger, shame, or lust we create perversion. Instead offer your addiction into the fire and incinerate it once and for all. Some people do this when they break up with a partner or leave a job. They take everything that reminds them of that person or place of employment and literally burn it up. This helps to cut the cord of attachment.

### ◈ THE FIRE CEREMONY

If you have a fireplace or backyard fire pit you can offer your habits into the fire, as represented by ghee or a ghee-soaked piece of paper on which you've written down what you'd like to release. Don't utilize a barbecue or fire pit where food is cooked. Your kitchen fire and sacred fire have separate functions. Keep them that way.

If you don't have a fire pit you can do this practice mentally. Sit quietly and imagine yourself making offerings into the fire, saying a prayer and reciting the Agnihotra mantra in Sanskrit or in your language. Those recitations are as follows:

Morning Agnihotra (fire ceremony):

*Suryaya svaha* (Oh sun, I offer to you)

*Suryaya idam na mama* (Oh sun, this is not mine)

*Prajapataye svaha* (Oh Lord, I offer to you)

*Prajapataye idam na mama* (Oh Lord, this is not mine)

Evening Agnihotra (fire ceremony):

*Agnaye svaha* (Oh fire, I offer to you)

*Agnaye idam na mama* (Oh fire, this is not mine)

*Prajapataye svaha* (Oh Lord, I offer to you)

*Prajapataye idam na mama* (Oh Lord, this is not mine)

## A Monk's Life

A big reason spiritual people take vows of celibacy is to cut the lineage of suffering—to not pass their "stuff" on to their children and prolong the cycle of ancestral karma. When a monk or nun takes a vow of celibacy they effectively say, "I take responsibility for all my stuff—it ends here with me! I am devoting my life to clearing the karmic baggage associated with this existence." This is a big commitment, requiring time, energy, and dedication, which is why the spiritual life is a full-time job. Just as normal folks work nine-to-five to sustain their material existence, so the dedicated monks and nuns, yogis and yoginis for whom the spirit is everything, work full-time on their job—enlightenment. Though you may not be ready for this level of commitment, your mirror will shine brighter when you clear the junk left there by your family. "If anyone comes to me and does not hate father and mother, wife and children, brothers and sisters—yes, even their own life—such a person cannot be my disciple" (NIV, Luke 14:26). Burning the bonds of ancestral karma begins with a desire to improve your life. Verbalizing and materializing that desire is the next step, covered in chapter 6.

# 6
# Sacred Sound

The universe is vibration. The essence of vibration is sound, and the essence of sound is language. In the previous chapter I also told you that the essence of language is mantra—prayer, poetry, and invocation. The word *mantra* is derived from the Sanskrit root *man,* which means "to think," and *tra,* which means to "transcend" and "protect." That which protects the mind is a mantra; that which transcends the mind is also a mantra. But there are tens of thousands of mantras in many different languages. How do you know which is right for you? What's more, how do you know what is a mantra and what isn't?

## THE WORD I KNOW

Mantras don't have to be in Sanskrit, Hebrew, or Hindi. They are the words you speak every day in the language you know. Mantras can be positive or negative; single words, phrases, or even names. That's why it's important to select a name according to the right principles—one that fits who you are and who you want to be, since the mantra we hear most in life is the sound of our name.

The advantage of mantras in ancient languages such as Sanskrit or even Latin is that people have been reciting them for thousands of years. By chanting them yourself you can tap into the standing wave of energy built up over the millennia by seekers from these traditions. The disadvantage is that most of us don't speak these languages today. They are hard to understand and often harder to pronounce. That's why it's sometimes best to start with the words you know—words organized in a powerful way to produce results.

---

### Finding Your Lucky Name

Vedic astrology has been used for many things over the centuries, one of which is finding your "lucky" sounds for personal, spiritual, and even financial gain. In astrological parlance this could be where your moon, ascendant, or eleventh cusp falls. If this means nothing to you, don't worry! A clever Vedic astrologer should be able to reveal these to you. In earlier times such sounds were used to name babies and give them a boost in life, matching their personality to their name. The mantra we hear most is our name: it makes sense that it truly belongs to us!

---

## A Simple Prayer

Let's start with a Western approach to prayer and mantra—getting something we want. Mantras are examples of active meditation in that people typically practice them with a goal in mind—to generate prosperity, calm the mind, invite spirituality, or attract a partner. Active meditation is an example of *you talking to the Source*. Passive meditation is the opposite: *sitting and listening to the Source with no active agenda*. Both active and passive meditation are crucial for cultivating your spiritual life.

If you feel uncomfortable chanting foreign-sounding words, or just don't feel connected to them, starting with an invocation in English may help you not only tap into your spiritual nature but also affect your material reality as well. Seeing this stuff work in daily life will further reinforce your practice.*

---

*My deepest thanks to Barbara Roberts, author of *Face Reading: How to Know Anyone at a Glance* (Healing + Insight Publishers, 2009), for introducing me to this mantra. Visit her website at www.facereading1.com.

Using the following sentence as an invocation, let's complete the missing spaces together. "I . . . (*insert your name here*) NOW DRAW . . . (*insert your goal here*) IN DIVINE ORDER, QUICKLY, EASILY, AND IN PEACE. IT IS DONE/AMEN."

This special mantra is arranged so that every element has a purpose.

**I:** All rituals must invoke the speaker for whom the effects are intended. By saying "I" you localize the invocation, making it specific to you.

**[YOUR NAME]:** Inserting your name further localizes your mantra to the space/time event that you are. You are telling the universe that the limited entity identifiable as "Mary" is doing the asking. This is important, as you likely want your results localized so you can experience them not as "concepts" you only imagine or dream.

**NOW:** This powerful mantra, effective in sales presentations and pep rallies, also taps into the basic reality of existence, which is that *time is an illusion*. "NOW" is all there is, and present-moment awareness is the gift of an evolved consciousness. Once you've localized yourself in space ("I, Mary"), pronouncing "NOW" localizes you in time. This minimizes the distance between you and what you are drawing to you.

**DRAW:** This is an action word that invokes gravity, the all-attractive force. To "draw" means to irresistibly pull toward you, just as gravity pulls you in and never lets go. It is even stronger than to "attract," since you can attract something but it may still not come to you. When you draw someone or something they have no choice but to approach.

**[INSERT PURPOSE]:** A common purpose is "my life partner" or "my right profession." You can even say "a hundred thousand dollars" if you want to be specific! But in some areas being specific is not necessarily better. For example, by saying "I, Mary, now draw my life partner . . ." you are specific to who is doing the action, but you are allowing the universe to determine the right object. We're not saying, "I, Mary, now draw Steve," or "I, Mary, now draw a tall guy who makes half a mil a year and drives a Lexus." Lists like this don't work. You can write a hundred qualities you want in a partner, but your soul mate may only have one or two of them. That's because your limited self cannot conceive of what is truly good for you. Let the universe give you what is right. Let go and let God.

**IN DIVINE ORDER:** This is the crux of the prayer. By saying "in divine order," you acknowledge, as Jesus did when he said "not my will, but yours be done" (Luke 22:42 NIV), that you are ultimately not in control of your life. You cannot will your heart to beat, your hair to grow, nor the seasons to change. These are in the hands of natural law, and by surrendering the natural law of your being you enter the flow of dharma. Dharma is divine order, and by following it you minimize negative karma. When you allow divine order to intercede in your life it brings you everything. Abandon it, and it abandons you. You can also say, "in divine love," particularly if you are drawing a life partner. This again ensures that it's not your personal love and interest being served but that of your highest self. The phrases "in divine order" and "in divine love" essentially invoke the same thing. Say what feels right to you.

**QUICKLY, EASILY, AND IN PEACE:** This summarizes the invocation, reiterating that everything you ask for should create peace, not strife. If worded properly and recited with devotion, it should produce results quickly and efficiently.

**AMEN or IT IS DONE:** This is the closing of the prayer, and it can even be in Sanskrit if you wish—*tathaastu,* which means "so be it". Every prayer must have an opening, a closing, and be repeated a certain number of times. Begin with nine repetitions daily, but for faster results you can do this mantra 108 times daily for a few weeks, until it begins to hum with power. Then, just by saying it once it will kindle the energy of your desire.

## SANSKRIT MANTRAS

The best way to know if a mantra is right for you is to receive it from an enlightened preceptor. If you don't have a guru or someone you can trust, you can experiment with different mantras to see what fits. You can also consult a capable Vedic astrologer, who should be able to give your sacred sound and point you to the right mantra for your specific time and circumstance. Some people stick with the same mantra for a lifetime—especially if it's enlivened and passed to you by a guru in classic *diksha* (initiation) tradition. However, for other people their mantras, like exercise routines or diets, can change over the course of a lifetime; what you need today may not be the same that works for you ten years from now.

Below are some Sanskrit mantras for different occasions. They've been around for thousands of years, and I've used them myself. Pronouncing them may feel like chewing on sand at first, but try them out to see how they can sanctify every aspect of your day.*

### *Mantra for Eating*
Here is a mantra to recite once before every meal.

> *Brahmarpanam brahma havir, brahmagnau*
> > *brahmana hutam*
> *Brahmaiva tena gantavyam, brahma karma*
> > *samadhina*

> "Spirit is the spoon and spirit the offering; by spirit
> > it is offered to spirit in the fire
> Spirit alone is the goal to be reached by those
> > absorbed in the work and offering of spirit."

The goal of eating is to transform something outside of you, like a carrot, into something inside you, like red blood cells, bone marrow, and brain tissue. Converting a carrot into brain tissue requires the fire of metabolism, called Agni in Sanskrit. Ultimately all elements come

---

*You can hear me reciting each of these mantras at http://spirittype.com/secrets-sacred-sound.

from Agni—primordial fire. From a scientific standpoint we are all stardust—produced from the elements churned in the bowels of the stars. We are all one—this is as much a spiritual as a scientific truth.

This prayer affirms that reality by equating consciousness/spirit with the fire, the priest, and the offering. These are also metaphors for the process of eating—the offering is the food, you are the priest, and the fire is your metabolism. The end goal is Brahma—consciousness. Recite this mantra to sanctify your meals, turning even a humble repast into a feast.

### Mantra for Instances of Death and Calamity

The Maha Mrityunjaya (Great Victory Over Death) mantra is a powerful mantra to recite during hard times, such as when you or a loved one is sick or when someone is dying. It is useful for averting premature death and is a powerful daily practice. Dedicated practitioners recite it 108 times daily.

> *Om tryambakam yajamahe, sugandhim pushti*
> *vardhanam*
> *Urva rukam iva bandhanan, mrityor mukshiya*
> *mamritat*

"We honor the three-eyed one, who is fragrant and
increases our welfare.
Like a cucumber from the vine, free us from the
bonds of death, but not from immortality."

This mantra first appears in the Rig Veda—perhaps the oldest scripture in the world. Its roots go deep, and practicing it daily can bring comfort in times of stress. A mother told me the following story.

*I was sitting watching TV one day when a sense of dread suddenly overwhelmed me. I was worried about my son so I stopped everything and began chanting the Maha Mrityunjaya mantra. I thought of his face and chanted—I don't know how long, maybe an hour or two. A few days later he called me and told me how he had been driving on a narrow highway when a car veered from the opposite lane into his. He swerved at the last minute and narrowly missed plunging his car off the cliff to a certain death.*

*I was stunned. I asked him when and what time it happened. It was the same day and time that I was chanting the mantra!*

## Mantra to Cook By

Here is a simple mantra to recite while cooking or preparing medicine.

*Achyuta Ananta Govinda*
(pronounce the first two names together as "achyutananta govinda")

*Achyuta* means "steadfast, immovable, firm." *Ananta* means "infinite, endless, eternal." *Govinda* stands for the chief herdsman, one who gives pleasure to the senses.

These are three names of Vishnu, the form of Spirit responsible for preservation. Food and medicine are designed to preserve our health and help us carry out our mission on this planet. Invoking the energy of Vishnu is one way to imbue the food and medicine we eat with energy to make us steady, long-lived, and fulfilled until the end of our days.

## YOUR PERSONAL SACRED SOUND

Ayurveda proclaims three body/mind types—Vata, Pitta, and Kapha.*
Each has a "seed" sound (*bija* mantra) associated with it: *aim, hrim,* and *klim* (pronounced "I'm," "hreem," and "kleem"), respectively. In addition, you have a constitutional sound indicated by the placement of the moon and your ascendant in the horoscope. There are 108 such sounds, and a look at your chart will reveal which one's are for you. Combining these—your ayurvedic seed mantra and astrological sounds—you arrive at your own personal, customized mantra.

For example, let's say you are primarily a Pitta type. This means that your "seed" sound is *hrim.* Let's also say that your astrological sound is *ga.* To complete your customized mantra, you must nasalize the *ga,* turning it to *gam,* then add *om* to the beginning and *namaha* to

---

*To find your ayurvedic body/mind constitution, please visit www.ayurveda.com.

the end of the mantra: *om hrim gam namaha*. If you want to add your second constitutional sound, you can. If you are a Pitta primary and Vata secondary person, with *ga* as your astrological sound, your mantra would be *om hrim aim gam namaha*.[1]

If none of this makes sense, it may be worthwhile to book a one-hour session with a qualified practitioner who can read your life map and help you find your personal mantra.

## TALKING WITH NATURE

Geniuses can be eccentric, and one of their qualities is talking to nature. How often have you seen people hashing out a difficult problem with, say, a tree, or the sky, or their dog? How often have you been on a walk and recited the lines of the speech you were giving the next day or the steps to an important problem you had to solve? This ability to "bounce" ideas off our environment, to anthropomorphize nature, is uniquely human and, in a way, uniquely genius.

Luckily for us our spiritual ancestors refined and perfected this habit of talking to nature. Though Consciousness, God, and Truth are one, its manifestations are many. We can access the Divine by sitting in nature and talking to the sun, the ocean, the trees, even the rocks and the breeze. Our ancestors formalized and made this easy with mantras, prayers, chants, and invocations. And though some religions poo poo this practice as pagan or even satanic, the truth is that their own prophets (from Muhammad to Buddha to Christ to Moses) found the voice of God—and enlightenment—in nature.

Perhaps the most ancient way to interact with nature is by honoring the sun. It is the one source of life and light around which every body in the solar system revolves, the effulgent, ancient father/mother without whom we perish in darkness—the true source of our enlightenment. There are few better metaphors for God than the epicenter of our existence. That is not to say that the sun in its scientific sense—the ball of gas, one among billions in the galaxy—is itself God, but it has the qualities of divinity. Invoking those qualities with ritual, prayer, and mantra is a great way to connect to the Divine in you.

## *Mantras to Honor the Sun*

As discussed, the best time to honor the sun is at sunrise and sunset. This is when we can look directly at it, even if for a few moments, without being blinded by its effulgence This is when the sun is most accessible to direct conversation via prayer, mantra, or silent invocation. Instead of Facebook, face the sun and let it give you its message.

> **Instead of Facebook, face the sun and let it give you its message.**

One of the foundational prayers of the Vedic tradition is the Gayatri mantra.

> *Om bhur bhuvah svah*
> *Tat savitur varenyam*
> *Bhargo devasya dhimahi*
> *Dhiyo yo nah prachodayat*

This simple mantra is recited at sunrise to honor the sun. You can repeat it facing east, sprinkling a teaspoon of water on the ground after each repetition. Or some practitioners repeat the mantra up to 108 times into a cup of water. That water becomes supercharged by their mantra, and they then drink it, imbibing its healing effects. You can do this using a copper cup or even a golden chalice for maximum effect.* This practice of mantra-charged food and water is part of the ayurvedic tradition, which offers alternative therapies for optimum health.

If you're brave you can recite the longer Aditya Hridayam mantra, which should be started on a Sunday and recited once every day, or at least every Sunday to honor the sun. It's usually prescribed if you have an afflicted sun in your horoscope or if you suffer from depression, heart disorders, eye problems, or sun-related issues.

---

*For more information on how gold relates to health and how to make gold water and other recipes, see *Sex, Love, and Dharma: Ancient Wisdom for Modern Relationships.*

# SIMPLE ENLIGHTENMENT
# WITH SO HUM MEDITATION

So Hum is an ancient mantra that straddles the space between active and passive meditation. That's because it has no desire associated with it. It means simply, "I am that." Like the biblical proclamation "I am that I am" (Exodus 3:14 KJV), it affirms that at your core you are simply Spirit.

## ◆ *SO HUM MEDITATION*

To practice So Hum meditation, in your mind say *So* as you inhale through your nose, and *Hum* as you exhale through your nose. Repeat. No sound is made—this is simply in your mind. Observe the breath going into your nose, down into your belly, then outside of you about twelve inches. Or simply watch and feel the tip of your nostrils as the breath goes in and out. So Hum meditation is the inner observation of your breath accompanied by mental repetition of *So* on the inhale and *Hum* on the exhale.

There is no set number of repetitions or time limit. Repeating *So Hum* and watching your breath is the bridge between active and passive practice. You can do it anytime—after breathing exercises, before sleep as you're lying in bed, or even while riding the subway. *You are that.* Remembering your essential nature wherever you go is the real goal of mantra.

### *The Sacred Blanket*

Setting aside time to chant a mantra or prayer is a great way to build a standing wave of purity that hangs with you all day long. But you don't have to limit your sacred sounds to the meditation room. Cultivating conscious speech all day is a way to honor yourself and those around you. The best way to do it is to understand your dharma type, which we cover in chapter 12. Speaking your truth in the way that's right for you helps you vibrate to your true essence. (If you can't wait to see how, you can take a peek on pages 122–23. Go ahead, I don't mind.) Another trick I use to go into instant meditation is to sit on one blanket every time. I've been using the same wool blanket for more than fifteen years, and being on it gets me immediately relaxed. Your environment absorbs the spiritual energy you create with mantra and meditation. This includes your altar: place items there that evoke and trigger your spiritual nature. Particularly useful are pictures of enlightened masters—gurus, saints, or other icons—whose image looks straight into your heart and tells you exactly what you need to hear in a language beyond words. These triggers—a sacred blanket and a holy picture—are profoundly useful shortcuts to help you center into your practice. Another is movement, which we'll take a look at in chapter 7. Practicing fifteen minutes to an hour of sacred movement before sitting to do a mantra or meditation will put you in that sacred state even more quickly.

# 7

# Sacred Movement

So far we've discussed easy ways to clean your inner mirror, like waking up early, deep breathing, and eating an enlightening diet. Exercise done right, or sacred movement, also does the trick. Sacred movement helps to lighten your body by eliminating waste and filling you with energy. Tamas (spiritual darkness) is heaviness and stagnation—it is countered by movement and friction.

## VARIOUS TYPES OF SACRED MOVEMENT

Over the ages different cultures developed unique forms of movement to create this friction. These include yoga, the many martial arts, and the even more varied forms of dance. Among these practices circular movements of the hips are integral for women, while explosive movements are specialized for men.

> Circular movements of the hips are integral for women, while explosive movements are specialized for men.

From our galaxy's spiral of stars to flowers blooming on Earth, nature flows in curvilinear patterns. As embodiments of nature women are encouraged to follow that flow by moving in a circle, something emphasized in dances such as hula, salsa, and belly dancing. Moving the hips also encourages a trim and agile midsection, which these cultures associated with beauty and health. Nature, besides being curvy, likes to dance. Include dance in your life to invoke Nature's raw and graceful power into your body, especially if you are a woman.

Squatting is another vital movement for women as it is the optimal position for elimination and for giving birth. Training to squat encourages open hips, strong legs, and a healthy GI tract, since squatting massages the digestive organs and encourages the proper downward flow of energy, called *apana* in Sanskrit. This downward energy assists with proper digestion, defecation, urination, and childbirth. By sitting in chairs, not walking (or dancing) enough, breathing shallowly, and consuming an improper diet, apana becomes stagnant.

Yoga was developed to encourage the proper movement of downward energy so that yogis would be able to sit for hours without disturbance. In fact the word *asana* means "seat," and the first yoga asanas were simply meditation postures.* Yoga and its various squatting movements along with dance and its circular hip movements are the best forms of sacred exercise for women.

> Yoga and its various squatting movements along with dance and its circular hip movements are the best forms of sacred exercise for women.

For men the best exercises include pressing movements like push-ups as well as explosive high-intensity training. A man's job is to "push away" unwanted intruders and protect his family. Push-ups develop this "pushing away" ability. Indeed, a strong, well-developed chest has always been a sign of archetypal masculinity. Explosive movements like the kettlebell swing or jump squat stimulate the thrusting motion of a man's hips, helping to boost testosterone, burn fat, and mimic the movements of both love and war.† This motion is essential for transferring force in activities such as throwing a punch, racing after an animal, or tackling an opponent.

---

*The original yoga asanas, as described in the *Hatha Yoga Pradipika* and *Shiva Samhita*, mention no standing postures, the main asanas being *padmasana* (lotus pose), *siddhasana* (accomplished pose), and *svastikasana* (auspicious pose).

†To see these exercises performed, visit www.spirittype.com/sacredmovement.

Explosive movements for men like the kettlebell
swing or jump squat train the motions
of both love and war.

For both men and women the best exercises are functional, incorporating movements human beings need to survive. Walking and running, for example, are vital for practically every species on the planet, since they are the primary means by which most animals gather their food. Early humans ran enormous distances to chase down prey. They also walked hundreds if not thousands of miles during migrations. To make these primal movements sacred, try incorporating the deep breathing technique taught in chapter 3 along with them. This will bring more oxygen to your lungs as you run or hike, while helping to detox your body. It will also make you sound like you're in labor. Don't sweat it; just explain what you're doing to your friends.

Have you ever heard someone soundly asleep breathe so loudly they woke you up? I'm not talking about snoring—just really deep, unconscious breathing. That's what your breath should sound like, at least for a few minutes, as you exercise. Besides the physical benefits, focusing on your breath during exercise helps you go deeper, turning fitness into a spiritual experience.

## Yoga for Your Type

The yoga tradition you follow as well as your skill level typically determine which poses you can practice. But knowing how to customize these according to your dharma type can help you zero in on which movements best suit the needs of your body, mind, and soul. In chapter 12 we'll discuss the dharma type—your customized software for finding everything from the best job to the best yoga pose. Below are the asanas each type should include in their practice.

For **Educators,** emphasizing the head in positions such as Headstand and Shoulderstand is primary. Other poses to incorporate are all standing balance poses that wake up the nervous system, like Eagle or Tree pose, as well as Warrior I, II, and III.

**Warrior** dharma types should emphasize strength poses, especially those involving the arms, like Peacock, Wheel, and Handstand. Fierce and difficult postures are also par for the course (Chair, Warrior), but Warriors should also throw in Educator postures like Tree or Headstand for balance.

**Merchants** need to focus on the midsection and its digestive organs. Therefore, abdominal strengthening postures like Boat, trunk-strengthening movements like Bow, or twisting asanas like Fish or Triangle are optimal. Merchants evolve into Laborers, so incorporating forward bends like Child pose and Downward Dog also help to keep them humble. Merchants generally do well with seated or lying postures.

**Laborers** do well with poses in which their feet or calves are stretched, like Hero, Child, and Downward Dog. Hip-openers like Bound Angle pose and Maha Mudra, as well as the wind-relieving postures, also work wonders for them, since the colon is the quintessential Laborer organ. All squatting poses like Garland are also great.

**Outsiders** benefit most from Corpse pose; the recumbent meditation position. Practices like yoga nidra, hypnosis, or visualizations that can be done in this pose work wonders for the typically anxious Outsider. Lotus is ideal for seated postures, and generally innovative or difficult positions are favored by the Outsider personality. The Outsider organ is the skin, and skin-to-earth contact is great for them. We give and receive affection through the skin. Babies born without touch and human contact have much higher mortality rates. Anxious Outsiders need to honor their skin with more frequent oil massage, physical touch (such as hugging), and lying asanas that encourage floor-to-skin contact.

---

## TO SWEAT, OR NOT TO SWEAT?

Ayurveda is the Vedic tradition that deals with human health. Ayurveda stresses working smarter not harder, recommending regular training at 50 percent of maximum resistance. This means that if you can do ten push-ups at a time, you should only do five, but do them more often. If you can perform twenty kettlebell swings, do ten, but do them throughout the day, with ample rest in between. This is an excellent way to build strength.

In modern parlance this is called "greasing the groove"—training to well below failure but doing it often enough so that your body becomes supremely efficient. This is what gymnasts do—body weight exercises at submaximal quantity but at a higher frequency. The reason behind this form of training comes from ayurveda, which says that one should only break a light sweat. A bit of dampness in the armpits or on the forehead is the signal to stop. Even if you do high-intensity movements, perform them only until you feel a bit of sweat appear on your brow. Then rest a full ten to fifteen minutes before repeating. This is greasing the groove and an appropriate Vedic way to train.

If you prefer to be a little more active in your training, or if you don't have time to take fifteen minute breaks between sets as suggested by ayurveda, you can practice being "sacred and sweaty" by doing any form of exercise to which you bring reverence, even if it makes you sweat buckets. Reverence means that your attention is on what you're doing, not on your laundry list. You are focused in the present, not the past or future. A great way to do this is to breathe intentionally. Whatever breathing technique you do, let the breath bring you back to your body. I like the deep breathing discussed earlier. So what if you sound like an elephant in labor? After all, deep breathing is a big reason to do physical activity, as it forces your body to clear out toxins and bring in fresh oxygen.

---

### "Sacred and Sweaty"
### Forms of Sacred Movement

**Running/Walking:** Running and hiking are the original exercises. They are primal to practically every species on the planet. Practice deep breathing while you run or hike to make it sacred and sweaty.

**Squatting:** Long periods of squatting help to open the hips and create lower body strength. In India to this day you will see men and women squatting while working or eating. This ancient practice is good for preparing the body for childbirth as, in opening the hips, an optimal angle for elimination is created. Most ancient cultures squat to defecate, thereby creating fewer lower GI tract problems like hemorrhoids, constipation, pelvic organ prolapse, bloating, and irritable bowel syndrome.

**Dance:** Again, the most artistic and ritualized form of sacred movement is dance. Dances like hula, belly dancing, and Latin dances such as salsa also honor the curvilinear patterns found in nature.

**Martial Arts:** Martial arts ritualize movement by honoring the teacher and respecting one's fellow practitioners. All martial arts sessions are opened and closed with invocations that bring awareness to what you're doing, making them both sacred and sweaty, especially for men.

**Yoga:** Yoga is intelligent movement. Unlike random stretching and exercise, its sequences are designed to evoke the sacred and sweaty in you by ritualizing your movements, cultivating your energy, and grounding you in the body. Squatting motions along with deep flexibility make this especially vital for women.

The next key to making any exercise sacred is to follow the proper *post-exercise* protocol. That includes a brief stretch or foam roll session, followed by stillness. Even the most brutal exercise becomes sacred when solemnized by the following protocol.

## ◈ STILLNESS IN TRAINING

After exercise lie on the floor in Corpse pose (*shavasana*) for ten to fifteen minutes. You can lie on a yoga mat, but do not add too many props (pillows, etc.) as you want to feel the hard floor beneath you. You are not going to sleep but rather creating stillness in your body to integrate the sacred movement you've just performed. In fact *this* is what makes your movement sacred—lying in Corpse pose after every exercise session. It doesn't matter if you just finished stair climbing or a wicked biceps routine, the end should be the same—a gentle stretch for five minutes followed by Corpse pose on the floor.

It doesn't matter if you just finished stair climbing or a wicked biceps routine, the end should be the same—a gentle stretch for five minutes followed by Corpse pose on the floor.

The benefits of this practice are twofold. First, it creates stillness and purpose in your mind. Too often after exercise we walk around pumped up, euphoric, but with no real direction. Or we are so exhausted that the rest of our day is on autopilot. Lying still in Corpse pose is the cure for this uncenteredness. Shavasana is passive meditation—a way of *listening* to the needs of your body without interference from the outside world. After ten to fifteen minutes of lying still, your body will tell you if it's hungry or thirsty, if it needs sleep, or sex, or stretching, or a massage. You will also remember important tasks that you have been putting off. Your priorities will line up so that your day becomes productive, focused, intentional. You will get up from Corpse pose feeling reborn, fresh, unstoppable! Your day becomes *yours* to live, not a series of random events you just experience.

The second benefit to this practice is that by lying passively on the floor you allow your muscles, nerves, bones, and tendons to *integrate* the movement you've just done. Muscle growth, fat loss, and detoxification happen *while you're resting, not while you're training*! Exercise is the stimulus for change—stillness is the nexus where that change actually happens. Without stillness you will never enjoy the full results of training.

Exercise is the stimulus for change—stillness is the nexus where that change actually happens.

Everything in life is fasting and feasting. Exercise is a fast from stillness; stillness is a fast from activity. Honor this universal cycle by creating stillness after exercise to stay balanced. If you only move-move-move all day long you lose balance and become a scattered, superficial being. Don't be superficial—go deep and let your inner wisdom teach you. Borrow this easy practice from hatha yoga to make your training sacred!

# 8

# Inside Out

In this chapter I reference a number of studies demonstrating what common sense and our ancestors have known for ages—that being in nature is good for you. These studies show the wide range of benefits of vitamin D sufficiency (and the dramatic potential for increased mortality in vitamin D *insufficiency*). They also show that it's good to be in green spaces and have ample exposure to the elements. One such study is the PHENOTYPE project in Europe, which measures nature's effects on human health and happiness. The Positive Health Effects of the Natural Outdoor Environment in Typical Populations in different regions in Europe (PHENOTYPE) project is the largest European project on green space and health. It examines the possible underlying mechanisms (stress reduction/restorative function, physical activity, social interaction, exposure to environmental hazards) for the relationship between green space and health in four different countries in Europe.[1]

In spiritual parlance nature is inherently sattvic and spending time in it lets some of that sattva rub off on you. Remember this word from chapter 1? It means *balance, purity,* and *enlightenment,* and you can find plenty of it in nature. Yes, I know that tornadoes and hurricanes are less than ideal conditions for refining your Downward Dog posture, but then again, even emergency situations can be tools for self-awareness, helping you get down to what really counts. Let's take a look at how we can plug nature back into our lives, bringing some of that purity along with us.

# THE FIVE ELEMENTS

Our ancestors believed that nature was composed of five great elements. They warned that separating ourselves from the elements outside would isolate us from our own *inner* natures, leading to disorders in the body and the mind. But by intentionally reconnecting to at least four of these five great elements on a daily basis we can heal our physical, emotional, and spiritual wounds. Here's how it works.

## *Earth*

The earth element is everything solid in our experience, including the bones in our bodies and the bricks in our houses. Earth is security and stability, shelter and food. To connect to it is to ground yourself in this security. Try taking your shoes off every day for at least fifteen minutes to feel the sand or grass under your toes. Try sitting in the park, rolling around, or even playing in the mud. Feeling the earth on your body can remove your cares and worries and balance stress levels from hyper-red to cool-and-calm green. Here are some innovative ways to add the earth element into your life.

- Work with clay, mud, bricks, or stone. Especially for men, who archetypally are supposed to provide security and shelter for their families, getting in touch with the earth by moving bricks, getting dirty, and working with stone is great, especially if they work at a job that doesn't expose them to their rugged manliness on a daily level.
- Garden or landscape.
- Sleep on the floor (on a small mat or mattress).
- Cook a full meal from scratch. This includes long periods of standing but also working with food that comes from the earth.
- Try walking barefoot on the earth every morning. Postpone putting on those socks or sandals—even flip-flops are rubber, which insulates you from the ground. Get your feet dirty—even fifteen minutes a day will make a difference in your life, from better posture to improved emotional stability.
- Give yourself a mud facial or a full "mudding" experience.

- Go for a long hike or walk, or try doing mat yoga or Pilates.
- Lift heavy weights. No, that five-pound pink dumbbell doesn't count. Women, consider that as mothers you lift your toddler up and down dozens of times a day. Your toddler weighs upward of thirty pounds. If you can do a full squat, biceps curl, and a shoulder press with a thirty-pound toddler, why can't you do it with a dumbbell? Who has convinced you that "toning" means lifting no more than five-pound Barbie weights, or worse, the two-and-a-half-pound mini-Barbie setup? Take it from a fitness professional: Bigger weights don't put on bigger muscle—they make you stronger faster. Don't be afraid to use them.
- Drink minerals. Calcium, magnesium, zinc, and the little-known mineral strontium are essential for bone health (though never take calcium with zinc or strontium as they compete for absorption).
- Raise your vitamin D levels to at least 40 ng/ml but optimally up to 80 ng/ml. If you don't know your vitamin D levels, get them checked.

The earth element is security, and if you're worried about money or your place in the world, your bones and joints may show stress, which may manifest as lower back pain. Adding strontium, zinc, magnesium, and vitamin D (see the fire element below) to your diet will help rebuild your body structure and relationship to the earth.

If you're asking how supplementing with minerals leads to enlightenment, consider that this is just one way to bring awareness to the earth element in your body. It is a step to reconnecting with nature—the nature within you. Though not essential for everyone, if you're deficient in any of these minerals they may be essential for *your* well-being, from digestive health to proper sleep, which translates into improved ability to meditate and follow all of the other recommendations in this book.

### Water

There is no ritual without water and fire, just as there is no life without these elements. Fire represents light and transformation, and water is nourishment. Water is gentle cleansing; fire is harsh purgation. Both are necessary for physical and spiritual enlightenment.

Spending time in and around water purifies you within and without—body, mind, and emotions. It is not enough to take a shower every day—drippy tap water can't compare to the sheer quantity and quality of an ocean wave submerging you or pure rain sprinkling your head and body, or a waterfall gushing around you, stripping you of all negativity. Nature's water sources are the first choice when it comes to connecting to this element. Surfing, sailing, swimming, and diving all work. Lacking such natural exposure to water, here are some innovative ways to add this element to your life.

- In the shower fill a few large buckets of water and splash them over yourself. Like a waterfall this helps to cleanse your aura.
- Drink half your body weight in ounces of water. If you can't remember this, drink water until your pee runs clear. That's a good sign.
- Add a fountain in the northeast corner of your house. (For more information on why the northeast corner is good for a fountain, refer to *Sex Love, and Dharma* for a complete discussion of the principles of vastu.)
- Try cold water dips. From professional athletes to Himalayan yogis, dipping in chilly water is a way to banish inflammation from the body and enliven sattva in the mind.

### It's Cool to Be Cold

It's hard to be feel enlightened with inflammation raging through your body. Inflammation is rajas—heat, agitation, activity—which leads to tamas—degeneration, disease, depression. In fact many of the practices described in this book can just as well be called "the anti-inflammatory program."

Athletes use cold exposure to fight injury and inflammation. Yogis dip into icy rivers to clear their minds and return to present-moment awareness. It's hard to think about your laundry list when your body is surrounded by freezing water—there is only you and the absolute reality of the cold. Life extension experts practice cold exposure because it promotes longevity. There are many reasons to do it. Pick one of the following to add more balance to your day!

1. Start by ending your shower every day with thirty seconds to one minute of cold water. Your shower can be as warm or hot as you like, for as long as you like. Simply end it with cold exposure. Make the water as cold as possible for best results.

2. Try hot and cold showers as an added way to move congested lymph and combat inflammation. Start with a comfortable temperature for as long as you like, then alternate with thirty seconds of cold exposure. Repeat as long as desired, but do not overdo it.

3. Consider cold water dips. Some gyms have them, but if yours does not, try a swimming pool in the winter or a brisk lake or ocean dip. A minute or so is enough in the beginning to get the immune-stimulating and enlightenment-generating benefits. Reward yourself with a sauna or warm exposure after you're done.

4. For advanced practitioners, try working up to ten minutes of cold exposure in the shower or outdoors. This turbo-boosts the hormone- and immune-stimulating properties of the cold; however it can also create problems if you have not trained yourself to do it properly. If you suffer from health conditions such as bronchitis, please consult your doctor before practicing prolonged cold exposure.

## *Fire*

In chapter 2 we saw how getting up at or before sunrise can infuse you with harmony all day long. But exposure to the midday sun is also useful, particularly since the UVB rays that generate vitamin D in the skin only get through Earth's atmosphere when the sun is directly overhead, perpendicular to the horizon. In addition you have to expose at least a third of your body for fifteen to thirty minutes to get the full effect.

Perhaps that is why people feel happy when they're on vacation. In tropical climates close to the equator, where the sun at midday is pretty much always directly overhead, it's easy to load up on healthy levels of vitamin D. But during the winter, especially in latitudes above thirty-four degrees (Los Angeles and higher), it is nearly impossible to get enough vitamin D–producing sunlight since the sun is too low in the sky, even at midday.

Therefore take advantage of the summer's natural vitamin D–producing light. Of course, if you have sensitive or cancer-prone skin that burns under sun exposure you can minimize or skip this practice, but be sure to get your vitamin D through dietary supplementation.

Healthy vitamin D levels range between 30 to 100 ng/ml, with 20 to 30 ng/ml considered insufficient and anything below 20 ng/ml deficient. Though you're not considered clinically deficient in vitamin D until you hit 20 ng/ml or below, it is best to boost your levels to above 50 to get the most from this healing hormone. Even subclinical vitamin D deficiencies can show up as depression, low libido, low energy, diminished cognitive function, and more. If you can't get it from the sun, make sure to get it in your diet or as a supplement, and get your levels checked every year!

Here are some innovative ways to connect to the fire element every day.

- *Trataka:* gazing at a candle for fifteen minutes to half an hour. Sitting still, gently contemplate a candle at eye level. Don't stare or force it. This yogic practice helps to focus your mind and may help improve eyesight.
- Eat cayenne pepper, chili pepper, and other red, spicy food. This will increase the heat in your body, but be careful—too much can also burn you up.
- Gaze at the sunrise. Only gaze directly for ten seconds at a time, and never do it when the UV index is above 1.
- Try starting a campfire using kindling and matches. Or better yet, lose the matches. Go basic and connect to the raw power of the Earth and fire by sitting on the ground and vigilantly lighting and managing the fire without lighter fluid or a lighter.
- Take a vitamin D supplement, especially if it is sourced from sheep's wool (lanolin). In Vedic astrology sheep's wool is

associated with the sun. How did they know this sun-wool connection way back when? Who knows. Today wool is considered the finest, most absorbable source for natural vitamin D. Other sources of vitamin D, such as fish oil, present hazards like mercury toxicity in addition to being more difficult to absorb. If you are a vegetarian, sheep's wool is more acceptable than fish oil, though sun exposure is probably the purest way to get this hormone into your body.

---

### The Benefits of Vitamin D

*The New England Journal of Medicine* reported the risk of death for intensive care patients at 45 percent for vitamin D–deficient patients, compared to 16 percent for those with sufficient vitamin $D_3$. There is almost three times the risk of death for patients with low vitamin D levels. *"Vitamin D Deficiency in Critically Ill Patients."* www.nejm.org/doi /full/10.1056/NEJMc0809996.

Another study shows that optimal vitamin D levels were associated with a 90 percent return in functional outcome after a stroke. *"Serum Vitamin D Status as a Predictor of Prognosis in Patients with Acute Ischemic Stroke."* https://www.ncbi.nlm.nih.gov/pubmed/26184826.

Vitamin D levels have been linked to the accelerated death of beta (insulin-producing) cells in cases of diabetes.* *"1,25-Dihydroxyvitamin $D_3$ and Pancreatic Beta-Cell Function: Vitamin D Receptors, Gene Expression, and Insulin Secretion."* https://www.ncbi.nlm.nih.gov/pubmed/8137721.

Studies have identified associations between vitamin D insufficiency and a variety of mental illnesses, including affective, cognitive, and psychotic spectrum disorders. *"Vitamin D Insufficiency in Psychiatric Inpatients."* www.ncbi.nlm.nih.gov/pubmed/23852104.

---

*This section excerpted from John Douillard's website, www.lifespa.com.

Higher maternal circulating levels of $D_3$ in pregnancy are associated with lower risk of developing ADHD-like symptoms in childhood. *"Vitamin D in Pregnancy and Attention Deficit Hyperactivity Disorder–like Symptoms in Childhood."* www.ncbi.nlm.nih.gov/pubmed/25867115.

In another study with 218 postmenopausal women, the group that was supplemented with 2000 IU of vitamin $D_3$ a day had 37 percent less inflammation in the body compared to the group that received the placebo. *"Effect of Vitamin $D_3$ Supplementation in Combination with Weight Loss on Inflammatory Biomarkers in Postmenopausal Women: A Randomized Controlled Trial."* www.ncbi.nlm.nih.gov/pubmed /25908506.

An Austrian study suggests that the majority of female nursing home patients who were vitamin D deficient had a 49 percent greater risk of mortality compared to the group with the highest vitamin D levels. According to the author, "The data underscore the urgent need for effective strategies for the prevention and treatment of vitamin D deficiency, in particular in the setting of nursing homes." *"Low 25-hydroxyvitamin D is Associated with Increased Mortality in Female Nursing Home Residents."* www.ncbi.nlm.nih.gov/pubmed/22319037.

Another study shows that the normalization of vitamin D levels significantly improved the severity of fatigue symptoms of primary care patients. *"Correction of Low Vitamin D Improves Fatigue: Effect of Correction of Low Vitamin D in Fatigue Study."* www.ncbi.nlm.nih.gov/pmc/articles /PMC4158648.

A two-year study of vitamin D supplementation with fifteen hundred patients showed healthy sleep patterns were linked to normal vitamin D levels. The most significant changes were seen when vitamin $D_3$ levels were kept between 60–80 ng/mL. *"The World Epidemic of Sleep Disorders Is Linked to Vitamin D Deficiency."* www.ncbi.nlm.nih.gov /pubmed/22583560.

## Air

The air element connotes *movement* in body and mind because it relates to the brain and nervous system, which stimulate your leg muscles to run and your mind to race. It regulates *communication* both within your body and with the outside world via speech and writing. The air element also relates to *touch,* since the nerves that communicate sensation to our brain also respond to touch receptors in the skin. Massage, self-myofascial release on a foam roller, or yoga or Pilates on the floor are some ways to vicariously pamper the air element in your body. Here are some others.

- Balance. Practice standing on one leg or doing wheelies on your bike. Since the air element represents your nervous system, wake it up by challenging your proprioception—the body's ability to know its address in space. This will refresh your brain, especially after long hours of sitting in the office. In the previous chapter I showed you that balance poses in yoga are perfect for Educators. That's because they're intimately connected to the air element, a topic we explore again in chapter 12. Go ahead, stand on one leg. Try it, I'll wait.
- Deep breathing (see chapter 3). Not only do you get a point for breathing exercises in the 7 of 11 Method, breathing also counts toward your four elements. Nicely done.
- Try a "wind bath" by going sailing, flying, horseback riding, cruising on a motorcycle, riding your bike, or otherwise exposing yourself to the free flow of air. Hike to the top of a mountain, or go out on a breezy day to feel the cleansing effects of Aeolus (god of the wind) on your aura.

## Space

In the age of smartphone digital screens, where many of us find it hard to look up from our devices, it is even more important to step out of the digital box and widen our horizons. Creating sacred space in our lives begins in the body by fasting and clearing the GI tract (chapter 9). It continues by honoring and decluttering the center in our homes—the place of spirit (chapter 10). Finally, creating space means exposing yourself to the great expanses of nature. Try staring at the far horizon. Skyscrapers and strip malls in the way? Take a Sunday drive far enough away from the city to see the horizon in the four directions.

Or simply spread out a blanket, lie down, and look up at the sky. You know, like when you were little and life seemed full of promise. Staring into the vastness of space creates aspiration and wonder. And if you think daydreaming is for babies, think again. Einstein did it, wondering what it would be like to travel on a light beam, even while his schoolmasters admonished him. But Einstein forever changed the world, while his headmasters are footnotes in history. Give yourself permission to widen your horizons, and like a goldfish, your soul will grow into them, filling them with possibility.

Here are some more ways to integrate the space element into your life.

- Look up at the stars. During the day our vision is limited by sunlight on the atmosphere. But at night we truly gape into the vastness of space—all the way to our singular origin. Get an app or a good book and see if you can find the constellations, planets, or even the International Space Station as it zips by at 17,136 miles an hour. Our ancient forebears spent hours looking fixedly into the night sky, measuring movement and meaning in the firmament. We are their descendants, and we owe it to ourselves and them to continue pressing the limits of our knowledge and wonder.
- Take a walk alone in nature. Sitting alone in front of your TV watching National Geographic doesn't cut it. Spending time in nature's spaces by yourself creates space between you and society. It's good.
- Meditate. Yes, your meditation practice (chapter 4) counts for one point all by itself in the 7 of 11 Method, but you can also check off the space element on this list if you meditated today. By sitting quietly you have carved out space in your day away from work and family to be still. This is to be rewarded.

Our ancient forebears spent hours looking fixedly into the night sky, measuring movement and meaning in the firmament.

### Let Nature Guide You

*One way to profit from your time in nature is by setting an intention and allowing the elements to guide you to the right answer or give you insight into a difficult problem. Let me give you an example.*

*One of my hobbies is trying to predict the outcomes of horse races with the help of Vedic astrology. I use sporting events like these as a "laboratory" to determine if certain techniques work. That way, when I apply them to real-life clients and their problems, I have some certainty that what I'm using is going to work.*

*In June of every year the third and most grueling leg of the Triple Crown takes place—the Belmont Stakes. Every year I put my skills to the test to see if I can pick a winner. But in 2017, just a day before the race, I still hadn't figured out the victor. At the time I was staying at the Arsha Vidya ashram in the Pocono Mountains. There, behind the property, a beautiful half-mile hike winds through the lush and verdant territory. One morning something told me to set an intention for my walk. So I did, asking, "Give me an omen into who is going to win the race," as I took off down the path.*

*No sooner had I walked twenty yards than I saw a pair of deer who stopped what they were doing and fixed their eyes on me. I froze, looking back at them. There was something peculiar about this sighting, because it gave me a warm, happy feeling. I smiled and broke my gaze so as not to startle them and continued down the trail. Later, after returning from my walk, I remembered that I had asked for an omen—and there it was. Two deer—number two or eleven would win. These were also my favorite horses in the race. As it turns out, number eleven was scratched—removed from the competition—leaving only number two, who, of course, went on to become the victor in the Belmont Stakes.*

Honor the five elements in these simple ways every day and your inner nature will reflect nature's purity outside. Review the 7 of 11 Method in the appendix to learn how to keep track of your progress and further cement what you have learned.

# 9

# Life in the "Fast" Lane

This chapter represents the most foundational practice in this book. Why isn't it at the beginning? Well, it was, but my editors felt that talking about enemas, which I do at the end, was impolite for first impressions. But now that we have met and know each other a little better, do you mind if we talk about your gut? Trust me, Jesus wouldn't mind. Nor would Buddha or the great yogis because one way or another they all addressed it.

You see, a long time ago an enlightened sage named Patanjali defined yoga as "cessation of the fluctuations of the *mind stuff*." He wasn't just talking about the gray matter in your head but your entire nervous system, including the enteric nervous system in the gut. The *mind stuff* in your gut is responsible for much of what you think and feel. When you're pulled over for driving alone in the carpool lane those butterflies in your belly are your mind stuff activating. When you have a "gut feeling" about someone or you are constipated or ill, your mind stuff feels it first.

So what did yogis do to cease the fluctuations of the mind stuff? Meditate? Yes, but not as a first step. Yoga postures? Yes, but not as a first step. Before you close your eyes or twist into your favorite asana, there is a more primal practice, one not restricted to yogis and yoginis. Jesus did it, Mohammed did it, Moses did it, the Buddha did it—and it was good enough to put them in touch with the Divine. That practice is fasting, the oldest spiritual discipline in the world, and it can help you too find your spiritual center!

Fasting is an art. By creating space in your body, it will help create space in your life for the things you want, including loving relationships, a disease-free body, and prosperity in line with your highest ideals. How can fasting do this? When done intentionally and according to the directions in this chapter you can witness the results yourself: it starts by changing your chemistry and ends with transforming your consciousness.

Some people think you have to take drugs to change your consciousness. Others believe that motionless meditation, severe penance, or hours of ecstatic dance are necessary to slip into other states of awareness. While these techniques work, fasting is a simpler, more reliable method to alter your reality while never relinquishing control of yourself.

Fasting works by creating space in the gut, which in turn generates peace and tranquillity in the mind. When your stomach is busy digesting, it is hard to meditate, pray, or feel tranquil. When your belly's churning and you're passing gas it's hard to think spiritual thoughts, because the body is busy moving food through your gut and toxins out of it. That is because the GI tract is intimately linked to the brain and the hormones in our bodies.

The gut's enteric nervous system, also called the second brain, does 70 percent of the heavy lifting for the immune system, and gut cells produce over 90 percent of the serotonin in your body. Keeping it busy digesting your last meal means less time for the higher functions your gut performs. But when you press the reset button for 12–13 hours per day (intermittent fasting) or by taking one day a week (24–36 hours) to fast, you release the energy needed to digest your Big Mac for other things, like attaining enlightenment.

---

### The Yogi's Secret

One secret known to Indian yogis long ago is that the mind stuff starts in the gut. The villi in your intestines propel nutrients in a wavelike manner along the GI tract while absorbing, assimilating, and excreting what remains. This process is called *vritti*, fluctuation, and there is no end to it unless your gut is empty for at least a portion of your day. To that aim, yogis cleanse their GI tracts in any number of ways, including swishing water, performing enemas, purging, and vomiting. But the best way is fasting, because other methods require work and preparation—vritti—which is what you are trying to minimize. After centuries of testing, fasting is still the fastest way to enlightenment!

## FASTING IN THE TWENTY-FIRST CENTURY

While fasting has been around forever, science has made great strides in the past century to expose its many benefits. Studies have proved that animals (and humans) on nutrient-dense but calorie-restricted diets live longer, healthier, and more productively than those who eat normally and take vitamins and supplements.[1] That's right. It's often better to eat less than to eat more and supplement with pills. Natural health expert Dr. Joseph Mercola has said, "There is actually more science behind calorie restriction than any diet in the world today."[2]

However for most people calorie-restricted diets are difficult if not impossible to undertake. Because of work, family, and other obligations, or a sheer lack of willpower, most folks will find the benefits of nutrient-dense but calorie-restricted diets out of reach.

> **It is often better to fast and take nothing than to eat and supplement with pills and vitamins.**

### *Targeted Fasting*

The solution is targeted fasting. Once a week or once a month choose a fasting day and practice not eating for at least twenty-four hours—from dinner the night before to dinner the day of. If not eating anything for twenty-four hours seems scary at first, try snacking on fruit when you need to, or drink green drinks like chlorella and spirulina mixed with apple or other juices. This will keep your mind energized and your body nourished while giving your system a rest.

A twenty-four-hour fast includes your normal eight hours of sleep, so you're only really skipping breakfast and lunch. According to Vedic astrology Saturday is a good day to fast since Saturn rules discipline and penance. A customized fast based on your horoscope, called Upapada fasting, is also a powerful way to improve your relationships by creating space for love to enter your life. A Vedic astrologer can help you find your specific Upapada fasting day. Finally, the day of the week you were born is also an option, but practically speaking you can fast any day that works for you.

Our ancestors often fasted out of necessity for lack of food, and at other times in observance of spiritual injunctions. Ramadan, Lent, and Yom Kippur represent some of these in the Abrahamic religions. In India things are a bit more fluid. For example, followers of the elephant-headed deity Ganesha may choose to fast on *Chaturthi*—the fourth day of the waxing and waning moon. That means that two days every month they consciously restrict their eating. Likewise, Vaishnavites (followers of Vishnu in his many forms) may fast on *ekadashi*—the eleventh day of the waxing and waning moon. Whatever days you choose, stick to them for three months and you will see the results.

Sometimes fasting is thrust on us for health reasons. If you've binged on food or alcohol the day before it may be wise to abstain the day after. According to ayurveda, if you have white coating on your tongue, bad breath, or you are still burping last night's dinner, you should *not* eat until this has cleared. A twenty-four-hour fast done once a month, or if you're serious, once weekly, is a great way to allow your body to reset, especially after indulgence.

### Longer Fasts

When you've practiced the twenty-four-hour fast a few times you can extend it to thirty-six hours, with dinner being the last meal on day one and breakfast the first meal on day three. That means you go an entire day without food, sleep on an empty stomach, and wake up to a nice breakfast. Health perks like leaner abs and improved lipid profiles are enormous . . . not to mention the spiritual benefits.

Moses and Jesus (literally or figuratively) fasted forty days and forty nights—not for health reasons but to connect with the Divine. Afterward their faces shone with spiritual radiance. "When Moses came down from Mount Sinai with the two tablets of the covenant law in his hands, he was not aware that his face was radiant because he had spoken with the Lord" (Exod. 34:29 NKJV). You too can experience some of this radiance by doing an extended fast. Try going thirty-six, forty-eight, or seventy-two hours, and even doing a week-long fast once or twice a year. Modern science-based approaches like the Fasting Mimicking Diet® advocate five-day fasts supported by supplements and snacks that make the fasting easy while providing scientifically supported results.* This program allows you to eat and feel satisfied while tricking your body into thinking it is fully fasting. (**Please consult with your doctor before considering any type of fast.**)

For most people the first day or two of a prolonged fast is difficult, but after that, as your hunger shuts off, you begin to feel light and energetic, embodying the true essence of enlightenment: feeling good for no reason. That is partly because when you fast your body enters controlled autophagy—literally, "self-eating"—which is a good thing.

### Breaking the Addiction to Food

Sometimes fasting feels like dying, because at the micro level your body is digesting itself. It's a little death—and doing it regularly may keep away the big one. By preparing your body for extreme conditions it becomes resilient—capable of handling ever-tougher situations. By touching death in small ways physically you also grow spiritually and emotionally. Your personal limitations begin to fall away. You start to touch your immortal self, the one beyond the personality.

> Fasting is a little death—and doing it regularly
> may keep away the big one.

When going without food you witness your thoughts and attitudes change. And while you won't turn into someone else like you might

---

*ProLon and the Fasting Mimicking Diet are trademarks of L-Nutra. For more information, visit www.prolonfmd.com.

when you're drunk or high, you'll begin to see the parts of you that are addicted to food and sensation. When you encounter and resist hunger you witness your weaknesses and your lust and realize that you can be beyond them. You *are* beyond them. And while you cleanse, some of these positive changes become permanent, unlike the drug or alcohol experience, which always comes with a price and never leads to lasting progress.

Fasting also exposes just how out of control you are. Even those who think they are disciplined and self-aware are shocked by how much their lust for food and flavor rules them. Regular fasting allows you to break your addiction to food in particular and sensuality in general. Just as we have a sensual center below, we also have one above—the tongue and its desire for taste. My mentor used to say that the tongue is the upper penis/clitoris. Abstinence from food is like abstinence from sex—it gives you control over your life and immense appreciation for food and sex when you do enjoy them!

By breaking your addiction to food with intermittent or regular fasting you will feel more in control of your life. This detachment will extend to other areas, potentially impacting how you relate to dear ones, bosses, coworkers, and the people around you. Because food represents the basic elements of sustenance and security, by detaching from it you'll notice that you become less attached to material objects of success, the *things* in life that people cling to for security—like cars, houses, money, and titles. This doesn't mean that you don't enjoy them—in fact you *enjoy them more* when they are part of your destiny to experience them. You are simply not devastated when they're not around. This is tantamount to achieving equanimity, and as Krishna says in the Bhagavad Gita, *yogah samatvam uchyate:* "yoga (union or enlightenment) is tantamount to equanimity."

## The Twelve-Hour Miracle

Okay, if all this sounds great but the weekly or monthly protocol is too much to tackle at first, don't worry. You don't have to fast for twenty-four hours at a time to reap spiritual and health benefits. Try fasting twelve hours *every day*, between dinner the night before and breakfast the morning after. The word *breakfast* literally means breaking the no-eat period that started at the completion of last night's dinner. Count the hours between dinner the night before and the moment you sit down for breakfast. If these total twelve or more, you're on your way to reaping the blood sugar stabilizing, longevity-promoting, and cancer-fighting benefits of full-fledged fasting.

Studies of breast cancer patients showed that women who gave their bodies less than thirteen hours fasting time between their last meal the night before and breakfast the next day, were 36 percent more likely to get recurring breast cancer. In addition, women who allowed more than thirteen hours between dinner and breakfast without eating not only *slashed their cancer risk by a third* but also had improvements in sleep and blood-sugar control. The study concluded that "prolonging the length of the nightly fasting interval may be a simple, nonpharmacologic strategy for reducing the risk of breast cancer recurrence."[3]

However, while regular fasting of fourteen or more hours demonstrates excellent health and spiritual benefits, it may also predispose one to gallbladder problems and potential gall-stone surgery. Therefore, if you choose to fast intermittently, do so for twelve to thirteen hours a day, or if you do it for fourteen hours or longer, give yourself a day or two off from time to time.

Tamas, the opposite of sattva, is heaviness, impurity, and confusion. Tamas is the mud that clouds your inner mirror, and it also promotes cancer, depression, and immune-related diseases. It is often caused or provoked by overeating. By fasting you allow your body and mind to clear tamas and shine through with sattva, reducing the health risks mentioned above while promoting clarity, love, and understanding.

At first you may experience hunger in the morning. The solution? Eat earlier at night. By ending your last meal around 7:00 p.m. you can easily have breakfast the next day between 7:00 and 9:00 a.m., allowing twelve to fourteen full fasting hours. If your work schedule doesn't allow it or you don't mind skipping breakfast, then you can eat later at night and go straight to lunch the next day. Just like any exercise, you have to practice the twelve-hour miracle. Soon it will become second nature.

### Intermittent Fasting: The Next Step

In his book *The Warrior Diet,* Ori Hofmekler advocates time-restricted eating—not eating most of the day and feasting in the evening. Though this sounds like it would put on weight, when done right it is massively effective for shredding body fat and packing on lean muscle tissue. That's because it teaches your body to be a more efficient fat-burning machine. In addition, this type of eating carries the anti-aging, free-radical scavenging properties that all fasts provide. That is because our bodies have built-in survival mechanisms that know how to deal with food shortages by adapting and making our systems more efficient. And because this style of time-restricted feeding allows you to snack on small amounts of raw vegetables and other foods (see Hofmekler's book for all the details), this may avoid some of the gallbladder issues present with long-term intermittent fasts that allow nil by mouth during the deprivation phase.

Start the protocol by reducing your daily eating window to ten hours. That means that you're fasting for fourteen hours between yesterday's dinner and today's lunch. This way you get the cancer-fighting, sugar-balancing benefits outlined above. When you're ready, try reducing the feeding window to eight hours, then six, and eventually down to four hours a day. Some high-level athletes and fasting aficionados go a step further and eat only one big meal confined to a one- to two-hour window. Contrary to what you may think, they are mighty buff, lean, and energetic.*

If this doesn't make sense to you then you've probably swallowed the "calories in, calories out" dish that nutrition "experts" have been serving for the past sixty years. The truth is, as studies in calorie restriction prove, it is *nutrition* that counts, not *calories.* When your body is adequately nourished by macronutrients and micronutrients

---

*While fasts like the Warrior Diet allow some snacking during the day, please check with your doctor to make sure you are healthy enough before undertaking any fasting protocol.

you can survive and thrive on intermittent fasting (easy) and even time-restricted diets (harder to do).

If you've ever watched a child play all day on a peanut butter sandwich you realize that it's not only calories that count. Hormones play the major role in human growth and decay. That peanut butter sandwich hardly contains enough nutrients to power a child's energy expenditure—not to mention to grow its bones, brain, and body to the point that a child outgrows its clothes every six months. Why can't you do that as an adult, even eating twenty peanut butter sandwiches per day? Because you don't enjoy the same hormone cocktail you did when you were a kid.

But there is a way to restore your hormone balance to optimal levels, no matter your age. Fasting improves levels of human growth hormone as well as testosterone and other hormone profiles. Ghrelin is the hormone that makes you feel hungry, and it's released in response to food deprivation. Ghrelin increases the expression of brain-derived nerve growth factor, which is responsible for producing more neurons in the brain.[4] This is why many advocates and yogis who fast regularly report better memory and improved cognitive function. You literally get *smarter* when you fast—or at least you are able to access your innate intelligence, since fasting burns away the mud from your inner mirror.

Another physical benefit to fasting is reduced sugar intake. A therapist once told me: "Simon, sugar = pain." How right she was! The less sugar circulating in your body, the less damage to your organs, joints, brain, skin, and gut and the longer possible life span for the organism as a whole. In addition, the less sugar you consume, the more efficient your body becomes at using fat as a fuel, training you to be a better fat burner.[5]

Here's how to practice time-restricted eating.

- Work up to fasting twelve to fourteen hours per day (don't worry—this includes your eight hours of sleep).
- If you choose a longer fasting phase as described in Ori Hofmekler's Warrior Diet, you can snack on small amounts of

raw fruits and vegetables,* including beneficial herbs like parsley and oregano and superfoods like chlorella. You can have a piece of raw chocolate. Water and coffee are also allowed, as are good sources of protein such as grass-fed whey and raw cheese, but no big meals. Snacking means that you're never fully satiated—you simply grab a bite to appease your hunger and keep going.

- During the evening feeding phase eat whatever you like. Start with vitamin-rich foods like greens and superfoods, then move to proteins and fats, ending with carbohydrates (dessert!). **Please also note that these foods and times listed for the evening window are guidelines.** Follow your body's wisdom and adjust as necessary.

### Fluids & Fasting

As stated, you can have coffee during the fasting phase to blunt hunger and stay alert. However, *do not* drink coffee first thing in the morning or after you eat in the evening. This may dehydrate you or keep you up at night. First thing in the morning drink sixteen ounces of room-temperature water. However, because water nourishes the bicarbonate buffer in your stomach, this produces more hydrochloric acid, which will make you hungry. (If you have no idea what a bicarbonate buffer is, or why it makes you hungry, please see my book *Sex, Love, and Dharma.* Along with dozens of recipes you'll also find my favorite book section title ever: "Me and Bobby McGhee," a whole section devoted to coffee and butter.)

Be judicious with your water intake as well, especially early in the morning. Sip and swish it in your mouth before swallowing. This helps absorption, allowing you to drink less and get more benefit. Wait at least an hour before having coffee. Use coffee as an antioxidant-rich tool to keep your intermittent fast going during the day. Consider blending

---

*In my backyard I have a small garden and some fruit trees. During the day when I get hungry I wander about and chew on a few leaves of kale, or on an unripe pear. (By the time they're ripe the birds have gotten most of them!) Whether you live in the city or the country, you can take advantage of this in your own home by planting healthy greens and vegetables to snack on. There's nothing like plucking fresh greens grown from your own soil and toil.

a teaspoon or two of ghee with your coffee to make a cappuccino-style drink that offsets the negative side effects of coffee while oleating your GI tract. (You can skip this if you prefer a zero-calorie fast.)

When you start getting hungry consider drinking sparkling water. This will also help to give you a feeling a fullness while keeping you hydrated. Sparkling water gives a greater sense of satiety than water alone and can be enjoyed as a luxurious drink rather than something you just gulp down.

## FASTING DO'S AND DON'TS

### *What to Do While Fasting*

- **Nap:** During a fast your body may demand extra rest. Give it what it wants to quench its long-standing need for rejuvenation and repair. Allow plenty of time for napping, lounging, and sleeping. Doing so will also keep the hunger pangs away. When you feel too tired to exercise or even walk, take a nap. When we eat food and drink coffee to push on we mask the body's natural fatigue signals, further depleting our system. By fasting you allow your body to tell you exactly what it needs. If it needs rest, give it rest. For this reason fasting on weekdays may not be convenient if you have to work or do chores. But if you can take the day off and spend it tuning in to your body, mind, and spirit, you will find yourself rejuvenated for the week to come.

- **Shop:** Another way to spend your fasting day is to get out of the house and treat yourself with something nice. Go ahead, reward yourself, you deserve it! People are generally in a positive mood when treating themselves, and whether it's a tie, a new purse, or even just window-shopping, getting yourself something nice while fasting is a great motivator. After all, you are saving money by not eating so why not spend it treating yourself?

You are saving money by not eating so why not spend it treating yourself?

### A "Fast" Way to Save Money

To estimate how much you spend on food, in a notebook mark down everything you eat and how much it costs, for at least three days. Average out how much you spend per day. If you cook at home, factor in how much electricity and water and other elements or utilities you use to prepare and store the food. Factor in your time as well. What is your time worth? Ten dollars an hour? One hundred dollars an hour? All of this put together should give you a snapshot of how much you save by fasting once a week. Many folks in Western countries will easily save twenty to a hundred dollars or more. Multiplied by fifty-two weeks this equals thousands of dollars back to you every year. Fasting is the tax return you give yourself.

- **Journal:** Write out your thoughts. One of the highlights of fasting is incredible clarity of mind. Use it to write down your goals and inspiration—your future self will thank you!
- **Meditate:** Do spiritual practice during a fast. It comes naturally and is easier to do at this time.
- **Enjoy Nature:** This is perhaps the easiest way to spend your day, as you will be distracted from hunger by the exercise and increased sensitivity to the beauty all around you. Who knows, you may write a song or figure out that sticky problem you've been working on.
- **Chores:** Staying busy is another terrific way to keep your mind off hunger. When you're free from the burden of having to prepare, eat, clean up, and put away food, you will have *extra hours* in your day to devote to other things. Is there a neglected closet you could organize or a garage nook in need of sweeping? Now is the time! By cleaning up your *inside* space you allow yourself time and opportunity to spruce up your *outside* space as well—your living or work environment. After a few hours of this, if you are tired, you can take a nap. Honor your body's energy systems by giving it what it needs.

- **Exercise:** Feeling hungry? Try exercise! Movement not only distracts you from hunger, it also helps to clean your inner mirror at double speed. Take advantage of your fasting time to walk, run, bike, and squeeze extra toxins out of your system. If you experience hunger, light-headedness, or fatigue, consider exercise as a remedy. Light movement like walking, cycling, or yoga not only distracts your mind, it also redirects your body's attention to your muscles where it can do the job of clearing built-up toxins and rejuvenating your cells. As we have learned, when your body is unburdened from digesting food, it will focus on clearing microcellular debris and enhancing cell communication and nutrition, facilitating total body cleansing and laying the foundation for enhanced cognitive and spiritual awareness. If you want to do heavier exercise like vigorous yoga or strength training, focus on squeezing toxins out of the muscles as you flex, paying special attention to the abdominals. Doing core and ab-strengthening movements is excellent during a fast as it ensures that the fire in your midsection is burning while detoxifying your body.

### Agni: Your Metabolic Fire

*Agnim ile puro hitam* . . . These are the first words of the first great Vedic scripture, the Rig Veda. They begin with the word *Agni,* underscoring how crucial fire is to our existence. *Agni* means "fire" on all levels. At the cosmic level, Agni is the sun, without which all life perishes. It is also the Earth, whose molten core of superheated iron is the reason life is possible. Planets without fire in their bellies are "dead," unable to support life. The Earth is full of Agni and, just like a human being, when it runs out, it too will die. On the environmental level Agni is the fire we use to cook food and make tools and shelter. In our GI tract Agni is the enzymes, proteins, and peptides that help break down and assimilate food. Spiritually Agni is the subtle flame of awareness that when refined and focused merges with the light of universal consciousness.

## ◈ *LION FACE PUSH-UPS*

One of the benefits of exercise is the release of pent-up emotions like anger, rage, and sadness. To facilitate the release of these negative emotions try performing Lion Face Push-Ups. This exercise works for both men and women. If you can't do a full push-up, try it from your knees.

Begin in normal push-up position. Try to squeeze every muscle in your body, especially your butt, abs, and legs. Lower yourself down to the ground. As you push up, stick your tongue out, roll your eyes up, and exhale with a strong HHHHHHaaaaaa! You can find Lion Face shown on YouTube or in good books on yoga; simply transpose it to doing push-ups and you've got it. Of course, you can add Lion Face to any exercise, like squats or sit-ups, but it works especially well with push-ups. If you have pent-up frustration or feel hot and irritable, do Lion Face Push-Ups and you will immediately feel clearer. It's okay to have these emotions—it's not okay to let them destroy you by harboring them inside!

> **It's okay to have these emotions—it's not okay to let them destroy you by harboring them inside!**

### *What **Not** to Do While Fasting*

- **Computer Work:** Stay away from working on your computer as this sucks up energy and may make you hungry. Your brain burns sugar, and focusing intensely on writing (trust me on this!) or other computer work will make your brain work that much harder. You may also be extra-sensitive to the EMR (electromagnetic radiation) from your computer at this time. The purpose of fasting is to detoxify your mind and body. By working on your computer or phone, you expose yourself to radiation. Don't do it. Get outside and use fasting to plug into the miracle of nature's internet. It's worth it.

- **High-Intensity Physical Labor:** I personally love to exercise while fasting—it keeps my mind from the hunger in my stomach—but it may seem obvious to avoid some activities, such as lifting heavy items or using heavy machinery. It is critical to listen to your body and know which activities may be too strenuous for you to perform during a fast.

- **Activities with Potential to Harm Others:** Being the driver on a long road trip may not be smart. Especially if you are new to fasting, use caution and be careful not to overextend yourself.

---

### The Incredible Lightness of Being

*"What is the average person's most sacred place?" the mentor asks.*

*"Well, probably church," I offer.*

*"Wrong!"*

*I sense there's a lesson in this, so I try to get clever. "What about the bedroom?"*

*"No."*

*Oh, I see. This is one of those lessons that I'm not going to get the first or the hundredth time. So I lazily throw out some options: "Their workplace, the football field, the living room?"*

*"You're getting warmer, but still not there."*

*"I give up. What is it?"*

*He grins at me with a twinkle in his eye: "It's the toilet."*

*Good teachers like to shock. Partly because this snaps students out of everyday thinking. Partly because they too get bored.*

*"Huh?"*

*"The toilet is a place of refuge—from husband, wife, boss, kids . . . but also where you clean the inner mirror. There is happiness after a good bowel movement that you don't get from church sacraments and cable TV. It is the incredible lightness of being . . . in the toilet!"*

---

## A RIVER RUNS THROUGH HIM

For most people cleaning the colon is a straightforward way to experience their true nature, at least temporarily. The lightness of being that comes from a clean GI tract is your own nature, wholeness, and health shining through. The word for "health" in Sanskrit is *svastha,* meaning "self-abiding." To abide in your essential nature is real health. It begins with a clean colon.

In addition to eating enough fiber to encourage healthy bowel movements, yogis and ayurvedic practitioners go a step further and clean their colons with simple enemas. A saying in India reflects the understanding that you can tell a good yogi when the river runs through them. That is, a yogi is supposed to be able to walk into a river, bend forward and drink the water, swirl it in his stomach, and by performing special *kriyas,* or movements, send it out the back end.

While most of us don't have this kind of "quick transit" ability, or rivers we can drink from for that matter, we can access the next best thing—the enema. In ayurveda enema is the premiere tool for treating 70 percent of health disorders. Thus it makes sense that enemas are the way to go, especially in modern Western culture, which is rife with processed food and unhealthy eating habits that disturb the GI tract. The colon and its microbiome is the seat of our immunity. Long undervalued in the West, it has been the primary site of treatment in ayurveda for thousands of years.

> The colon and its microbiome is the seat of our immunity.
> Long undervalued in the West, it has been the
> primary site of treatment in ayurveda for
> thousands of years.

## THE AMEN-E

In addition to its health benefits, the enema offers a quick, "lazy" way to enlightenment by cleaning the inner junk from our bodies and letting the light of self shine through. This is the complement to the church's "Amen!" since *enema* is *amen* spelled backward . . . with an extra *E.* Traditionally, ayurveda recommends hundreds of enema recipes for different needs, but the queen of the Amen-E is *dashamula,* "ten roots" tea. In modern times, a simpler alternative exists—the coffee enema—and we'll see how to make it ayurvedic, safe, and effective. While fun to drink, coffee may be even more effective when taken rectally, as modern alternative health practitioners attest. A Google search of "coffee enema" will show you that it is used for everything from treating cancer to losing weight.

What they don't tell you is that it can also be a tool for enlightenment. Here's why: Performing enemas is a way to carve out some time for yourself. Creating space in your day is one of the hallmarks of spiritual discipline. No one became enlightened by focusing 24/7 on work or keeping the brain busy with TV, food, school, family, chores, and the other minutiae that keep us trapped in left-brain, problem-solving consciousness. Creating ample time for self-reflection is a must if you are to allow Spirit to shine through you. Making "me" time for enema therapy is one way to do that, since in addition, during the thirty to sixty minutes or so it takes to perform, carry around, and expel an enema, you can't do much else but focus on your belly. Belly-centered consciousness is one of the classic tools for self-awareness. It comes with no extra charge with your enema therapy.

Cleaning the colon also helps detoxify the liver and balances your gut flora, neurotransmitter levels, and more. Human beings are a bit like donuts—or eclairs—we come with a hollow center. Usually we've filled that hollow center with junk. By squeezing out the goo and giving our body time to rest we create space, allowing Spirit to enter. A full cup cannot be filled. An empty cup receives the ablution of Spirit.

Even if you're sensitive to coffee, as I am, you're not likely to feel much of a buzz when taking it rectally unless you use a massive amount. You can also add oil and herbs to balance out the negative effects of coffee. Adjust the dosage to your needs—from one to three tablespoons of organic, dark roast, freshly ground coffee to one to four cups of spring or purified water. Use less water if you want to retain the decoction longer—more if you want to expel quickly and get on with your day. Do not use instant or decaf—they don't have the same effect. *Never, ever, use tap water.* Use purified, distilled, or spring water instead.

> A full cup cannot be filled. An empty cup
> receives the ablution of Spirit.

##  CLEAN FROM THE INSIDE OUT
### How to Perform a Coffee/Licorice/Dashamula Enema

Ingredients:

> 2–3 tablespoons of organic, ground, dark-roast coffee
> (regular, not decaf), and/or
>
> 2–3 tablespoons dashamula (ayurvedic "ten roots"
> coarse mix), and/or
>
> 2–3 tablespoons cut licorice root
>
> ¼ to ½ teaspoon black salt, rock salt, or sea salt

1. Combine coffee and (optionally) the licorice or dashamula to 2–4 cups of boiling spring or filtered water. If you don't want to do a coffee enema, which can be stimulating for some people, use the preferred ayurvedic mix dashamula or if you can't find it, try licorice. If you have yeast overgrowth, or parasites, or imbalanced gut flora, also add a teaspoon of the herb vidanga (*Embelia ribes*). Vidanga kills bad bacteria and fosters the growth of good bacteria. It also helps difficult skin conditions like eczema and infections. (Vidanga, dashamula, and licorice are available from ayurvedic herb distributors.)

   If you don't have licorice root or powder simply add a few tea bags of good, organic licorice tea. Do *not* use licorice extract.[6] In its raw form licorice powder is quite safe. In its highly concentrated form licorice extract may increase blood pressure when taken orally, but even then, only in very high doses. You may also add ¼ to ½ teaspoon of Himalayan sea salt or (even better) rock salt to the mix. This is highly beneficial to the colon. You can also add other beneficial herbs like gotu kola, but don't get too fancy. Stay with coffee, licorice, dashamula, and/or vidanga. And don't worry, unless using massive doses of the raw licorice herb, this should not affect your blood pressure.[7]

2. Add salt and let boil for five to ten minutes, then remove from heat. Let it steep for twenty minutes then strain into a glass container. Use a tight-mesh strainer so no coffee or herb stuff gets through.

3. Let this cool sufficiently (test with your pinky finger) then pour into a disposable enema bag or a sturdier stainless steel enema bucket, both available from Amazon.com or your local pharmacy. Place some castor oil on the applicator

tip, lie on your *left* side, and insert rectally. Follow the instructions in your enema kit for the full procedure.

4. Once the liquid is inside, continue lying on your left side for five minutes. Then lie on your back or, preferably, invert into a bridge or shoulder stand to expose the concoction to as much of the colon as possible. Being upside down, comfortably, is a good way to let gravity do the work. It is important not to strain too much, however, so if these poses are difficult for you simply lie on your back for five minutes. Finish by turning to your right side for five minutes.

5. Once you're done with your morning "bathroom yoga" get up and walk around. Within five to thirty minutes you'll feel a pull to go to the bathroom. Don't ignore it. Expel the liquid and feel the incredible lightness that ensues. If you feel the impulse to expel almost immediately, follow it. Never repress nature's urges, as this disturbs the colon. Next time simply use less liquid, or make sure you have a bowel movement before performing the enema. But even a two-minute enema is better than nothing! If you have done your bathroom yoga you may not feel any impulse to release. This is called a retention enema, a result of the liquid being spread through your colon and absorbed in the body.

6. Do this one to four times per week for four weeks. Then reduce the frequency based on how you feel. You can continue a once- or twice-weekly or even a monthly maintenance regimen for the rest of your life.

## Sesame Oil

After the first week, or once your colon is purified, you should add one or more tablespoons of sesame oil to your decoctions for lubrication. Of course you can add this from the beginning, especially if you tend toward constipation. Raw organic sesame is the premiere substance used in ayurveda for nourishing the colon, feeding your microbiome, and calming nervous and GI tract disorders. It helps to blend the oil with your coffee or licorice decoction for maximum absorption. Here's how it's done.

1. Brew your coffee/dashamula mix and let cool.
2. Strain into a blender and add your 1–3 tablespoons of raw, organic sesame oil.
3. Blend for five to ten seconds.
4. Let it settle a few minutes before proceeding to your Amen-E.

By blending the sesame oil with your decoction you make sure the oil doesn't sit on top and gets perfectly absorbed. You're basically creating a kind of "bulletproof coffee" for your gut, improving its utilization and absorption.

Over time you can work up to using a 50-50 mix of oil to decoction. In fact ayurveda recommends oil-only enemas for added rejuvenation. But beware: if you're using a lot of oil it helps to do the enema at night, since oil "seepage" can occur during the day, which can be embarrassing! A rule of thumb to follow: do decoction enemas on an empty stomach (morning) and oil-only enemas on a full stomach (evening). This also helps you to retain the oil as long as possible, which is what you want when doing oil-only enemas.

The difference between decoction enemas (coffee and/or herbs and water) and oil enemas is that you can expel herb decoctions after fifteen minutes, but it's better to hold an oil enema once inserted. You would also use a lesser quantity of oil to encourage your body to retain it. Use only organic sesame oil, *not* the *toasted* sesame oil used in Chinese cooking.

> **A rule of thumb to follow: do decoction enemas on an empty stomach (morning) and oil-only enemas on a full stomach (evening).**

## *Amen-E Concoctions/Ingredients*

Aside from coffee and herbs there are multiple recipes you can make to clean and nourish your inner skin. Here are some I recommend.

### Bone Broth Protein and Collagen

You can make your own by boiling goat bones (best), or buy the bone broth protein/collagen powder sold in health food stores. Boil this with your licorice or other herb powders. This is perhaps the most powerful rejuvenative enema you can make, and ayurveda commonly recommends it for depleted nervous, skeletal-muscular, and reproductive systems. You can add a touch of raw, organic sesame oil to this for added rejuvenation. This restorative enema can help with joint and muscle aches, skin problems, and a host of other issues caused by stress and exhaustion. Try it and you will see why it's a favorite of ayurvedic doctors.

### Probiotics

Try adding one or two capsules of high-quality probiotics to your decoction after it has cooled. This will deliver these microscopic warriors directly to the inner battlefield where they will fight to restore balance in your kingdom. You can also use a tablespoon or two of yogurt added to your decoction. Mmm . . . coffee and yogurt. But beware: sometimes probiotics may cause pressure and gas in your colon as these bacteria go to work. Be judicious and don't do this if it's your first time performing the Amen-E.

### Honey

Adding honey to your Amen-E is nourishing to your system and helps feed the bacteria in your gut. In ayurveda a half-and-half honey and sesame oil enema is considered a prime rejuvenative, especially for vegetarians who do not use bone broth or animal products. Add one to three tablespoons of raw, unfiltered honey and the same amount of sesame oil to your lukewarm decoction. Blend well. Make sure your honey is *raw* and the decoction is not hot. Raw honey is nectar; cooked honey is poison. It is harder to retain honey enemas, because they feed the bacteria in your gut, which creates pressure to expel the solution. Stay close to a toilet!

### Rock Salt

As mentioned above, adding a natural, mineral-rich salt like black, Himalayan, or sea salt to your enema will help its absorption and efficacy.

## WHAT'S YOUR INSPIRATION?

The pick-me-ups you use to boost productivity say a lot about who you are and the quality of your work. As a writer I know that sometimes I need a boost to my inspiration. According to legend that's how coffee was discovered in the first place—by monks in Ethiopia who used it to stay alert during prayers.

My go-to snacks are sugar and sometimes coffee. But I've found that ultimately meditation gives the best results. You can often judge the quality of a book just by asking the author what they used as "inspiration" to write it.

If it's cigarettes and liquor, that work is going to be imbued with tamas and rajas qualities that produce hard, action-packed, and cynical material. If you're inclined to sweets like me, the qualities are mostly rajas with a bit of sattva, yielding soft, sweet, and sometimes limp material. When it's weed—marijuana—the quality is a lazy sort of tamas with a hint of false sattva, meaning that the person will think their stuff pure and enlightening, but it will ultimately not stand the test of reality. Other drugs like meth and cocaine increase the volume of tamas and rajas, increasing violence and cynicism.

If you're going to opt for coffee, as I have at times, consider going the route of the Amen-E: injecting it rectally and minimizing much of its negative effects while benefitting from its colon-cleansing and liver-flushing properties. Drinking a bit of caffeine here and there for alertness is also not a problem. But start to rely on it excessively, and it will burn you out. Ultimately, if you follow the 7 of 11 Method in this book every day, you shouldn't want for inspiration. Sacred movement, deep breathing, and the other practices are designed to stir your inner knowledge to come to the surface, rendering external stimulants like caffeine and cigarettes obsolete.

# 10

# Home Sweet Home

Your home should be a refuge, not a dungeon. Converting it into a sacred space and shelter from the world will help to lighten the load in your body and mind. Remember that *enlightenment* means both "to make less dark" and "to make less heavy." In this book we've seen how to create enlightenment in your body and mind with fasting, pure food, meditation, exercise, and other methods. Now it's time to sanctify your living space by putting the heaviness where it belongs and inviting light to shine where it's needed.

In chapter 5 of my book *Sex, Love, and Dharma: Ancient Wisdom for Modern Relationships,* I showed you how to use the ancient science of vastu shastra to balance your environment for improved relationships. In this chapter I'll show you the basics of making the most of your living arrangements for spiritual enlightenment. The rules are not so very different.

## THE BASICS

1. Keep the center of your house uncluttered and free of major furniture. Like your body's center, the gut, your home's inner space needs to be open to allow Spirit to enter.
2. Keep the northeast part of your home open and uncluttered. If you have windows here, undrape them. Install an altar or a water feature. Move heavy furniture and appliances out of this area, into the southwest.
3. If possible, create a positive doorway or entrance to your home.

## What Is Vastu?

This is one of the last Sanskrit words in this book you'll have to swallow. A vastu is a dwelling place. For example, your garage is a vastu for your car. Vastu shastra is the science of creating harmonious dwellings for humans, animals, and yes, even your Toyota Corolla. This includes the design of homes, cities, and temples for improved health, wealth, and enlightenment. Vastu shastra hearkens back to the Harappan civilization (3200 BCE) and beyond, which means that you have five thousand years of wisdom to draw on to find the perfect spot for your petunias.

## *Optimal Door and Window Placement*

Doors and windows are to a house what your eyes and mouth are to your face—the first thing people see. As such, they reflect the character of the entire home. If your teeth are yellow and crooked, no matter how noble you are, you will be diminished in the eyes of the world. If your windows are cobwebbed and dirty, the residents, no matter how bright, will experience diminished vision. Your body is a vastu for your soul. Your home is a vastu for your body. Let's begin by examining the optimal door placement for enlightenment and prosperity.

> Your body is a vastu for your soul—your home is
> a vastu for your body.

Northeast is the most sacred direction; keep it free and clear of clutter and try to put your entry doors and windows there. A vastu expert I know swears by this practice, encouraging homeowners to physically move their front doors if they are poorly placed. He claims recovery from illness, improved prosperity, and better relationships as a result.

I don't think you have to go as far as moving your door, but the benefits of these improvements may outweigh the cost for some people, while for others living with a west- or south-facing door may work just fine. Part of this depends on your astrological horoscope. Earth-sign

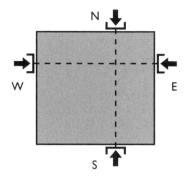

*Pick one of these vastu-friendly front-door placements to create a sight line (dotted line) moving through the northeast direction. Placing windows in the northeast opens your space to the same benefits.*

ascendants, for example, may do fine with a south-facing door since earth signs correspond to the southern direction. Air-sign ascendants may do well with a west-facing door since air signs correspond to the western direction. But for most people the northeast is the all-purpose safe direction.

> Northeast is the most sacred direction; keep it free and clear of clutter and try to put your entry doors and windows there.

## ASCENDANTS IN VEDIC ASTROLOGY

| ELEMENT | SIGNS | DIRECTION |
|---------|-------|-----------|
| Fire | Aries, Leo, Sagittarius | East |
| Earth | Taurus, Virgo, Capricorn | South |
| Air | Gemini, Libra, Aquarius | West |
| Water | Cancer, Scorpio, Pisces | North |

But what if you don't own your home or can't change the front door? If your house has a poorly placed door create an outside gate in the northeast (or one of the other positive door directions). This way when you enter the yard you are traveling through the positive door space. If you live in an apartment complex use the northeast entrance (if there is one) or one of the other positive placements to arrive at your building. In your mind, let this entrance be the "door" to your home.

## Respecting Fire

In chapter 8 we discussed the importance of the fire element and how to balance it in your body. Now let's look at how to honor it in your home. Southeast is the direction of fire; any water placements here diminish the health of the inhabitants according to vastu shastra. For example:

- Swimming pools in the southeast are to be avoided. If you already own one, build a brick wall between the house and the pool, or fill the pool in and cover it up.
- Toilets in the southeast diminish the fire element. If you have one, try placing a bowl of sea salt or pink Himalayan salt in the toilet. Change it once a week. You can also put a salt lamp or move the toilet to another room (but not one in the northeast).
- Septic tanks in the southeast are bad for the same reason. Move them to the east, northeast, or west direction.

Southeast is the optimal placement for a kitchen. There the fire element feels at home. If your kitchen is not in the southeast, consider putting a permanent fire fixture like a salt lamp in this corner and leave it on all the time. An alternate placement for the kitchen is the northwest, but avoid the northeast.* Given that cars have internal combustion engines, the garage is also okay in the southeast, as are all of your electronic devices like Wi-Fi routers, stereo equipment, and garage-band amplifiers. However, even in the southeast, these electronic devices can be harmful to your health if not properly managed, as we'll see below.

## The Placement of Water Features

According to my friend the vastu expert, a major problem in the home is the placement of water. I have seen vastu adepts like him walk into a house and diagnose family ailments on the spot with questions like, "Does your wife have cancer of the reproductive organs?" too often answered in the affirmative. The culprit may be the wrong relationship

---

*For more information about optimal room placements, refer to *Sex, Love, and Dharma: Ancient Wisdom for Modern Relationships.*

with water in the home. This includes swimming pools, water tanks, nearby rivers and lakes, and septic tanks, as described above. Generally these should not fall in the southwest, south, or southeast direction.

The optimal placement for these is in the northeast. The north and northwest are also fine, but actively avoid the southwest, south, and southeast. If you have any of these water features here do everything you can to move or fill them in, or again, at least block them from view with a brick wall. Coupled with positive door placement and an uncluttered center, this should go a long way toward ensuring your home remains a sacred sanctuary for years to come.

## *The Hazards of Electromagnetic Frequency*

We are awash in a sea of electromagnetic radiation (EMR) or electro-magnetic frequency (EMF), most of which comes from natural sources like the sun, space, and even the energy radiating from the cells in our bodies. But in modern times humans are exposed to increasing levels of artificial EMR.

If you could *hear* the frequencies put out by your computer, cell-phone, Wi-Fi router, and other electronic devices you would likely go mad over time. That's because the waves are so chaotic they approximate sound torture—something the U.S. government uses on inmates and potential terrorists!

Unlike your neighbor's Saturday-night broadcasts of death metal guitar, electromagnetic radiation is a 24/7 onslaught that you cannot easily avoid. You can't call the cops or reason with the offending neighbor. EMR is all around us, and a big part of creating sacred space in the twenty-first century involves artfully managing it.

Here are some tips for minimizing your exposure to harmful EMFs.

- Move your internet router outside your bedroom. Ideally, put it somewhere you don't spend much time, or in the southeast corner. If possible, don't use a wireless router at all—get cable internet. This means plugging your Ethernet cable into your router and connecting via cable to your computer. *You will still have to call your cable company to disable the Wi-Fi signal—it will* not *disable on its own!*

- Do not install so-called smart meters in your home. If your electric company forces you to, consider shielding the inside wall of your house where the smart meter sits by purchasing EMF-blocking materials.
- Do not carry your phone in your shirt or pants pocket. Keep it away from your body, especially when it is not in airplane mode.
- Do not put your phone to your ear to talk. Use a Bluetooth headset or ear buds.
- If you must carry your phone or computer, cover them with EMR-shielding devices.
- Unplug electronics you're not using at night. This means the TV, Wi-Fi, cable, charging devices, and others. Though not being used, if they're plugged in they're still emitting EMR.
- Do not use your phone while driving. The signal strength can be four times higher while your phone searches for a signal. In addition, since your car is a steel box, that signal bounces around inside, upping your exposure. Put your phone down in the car and drive! Doing so will keep you safer as well.
- If you live next to a microwave (cell phone) tower or an electrical substation, or very near large electrical wires, consider moving. The radiation from cell phone towers causes cancer. You may save some money living there because it's cheaper, but it's not worth sacrificing your health or spiritual evolution.
- Consider installing EMF-dampening devices in your home. In ancient times *vastu yantras*—special pyramids imbued with precious and semi-precious stones—were installed in homes to keep their inhabitants safe and sound. These days a version of the vastu yantra may be devices designed to shield your home from harmful EMR. Vastu pyramids may also help deflect negative EMR, though specialized devices for just this purpose also exist.[1]

Studies to date show correlation with EMFs to cataracts, autism, epilepsy, Alzheimer's, sterility in men, headaches, DNA damage, memory loss, ADD, immune changes, cancer, sleep loss, tinnitus, drug interactions, asthma, diabetes, and more.[2] For modern practitioners of vastu shastra, learning to artfully deal with EMFs is one of the challenges of living in the new millennium.

---

### What's My Karma?

*"What's the point of protecting your home if it's your karma to experience certain negative outcomes?"*

*Whatever your karma, whatever the horoscope says, if your home is vastu-protected you will suffer no ill-effects . . . as long as you stay in that home!*

*"But what if you can't deck your house out in perfect vastu style? What if you live in someone else's house or in an apartment, or you can't afford to move the front door to an advantageous position?"*

*Then your karma is fixed . . . and your horoscope prevails.*

---

## Unplug and Play

In researching my book *Gambler's Dharma,* I studied professional sports bettors and their habits. Spending time with experts taught me that the worst thing you can do for prosperity and good decision-making is to watch nonstop TV. The most successful investors, called *sharps*, had a disdain for amateur players, whom they termed *squares*. That is because squares rely on TV, hype, and emotion to make decisions, while the pros—the sharps—switched their TVs off and did their research behind the scenes, with little emotion or fanfare.

A TV commentator's job is to entertain and capture your attention. TV programming is designed to elicit primal emotions like fear and desire, to keep you glued to the screen. Whatever your passion—sports, investment, politics, or even movies—the worst thing you can do is watch TV all day long. It is nearly impossible to stay in an enlightened state while sitting through commercials or watching mind-numbing pundits argue. Even movies and DVDs, though great for unwinding, can be overstimulating if they're on all the time.

As mentioned earlier, a comment I hear a lot is, "The best decision in my spiritual life was getting rid of the TV." I challenge you to minimize your screen time for a month. That means going "dark," as far as that's possible in a digital world. Checking emails and working for up to an hour or so on your computer is probably fine, but don't overdo it. Give yourself a point in the 7 of 11 Method if you can "unplug and play" all day!

### *Additional Vastu Pointers*

- Mirrors or wall clocks should *never* be put along the south wall. The north or east wall is better.
- The stove should be kept clean and not placed under a window or next to the fridge or sink. A dirty stove blocks family finances.
- The dining table should not have a missing corner. Round, oval, square, rectangular, or octagonal tables are good.
- The kitchen should not directly face a toilet. If it does, keep the toiled door closed (duh!).
- It's preferred that the total rooms in the house (including bathrooms) be odd in number.
- In every room as far as possible more walking space should be left in the north and east directions.
- If renting out part of the house, stay in the south portion.
- Face north or east when studying or working; do not face south or west.
- Spend waking hours in the north and east and sleeping hours in the southwest.

To create sacred space in general, keep the center and northeast parts of your house light and free of furniture, appliances, and clutter. Protect yourself from harmful electromagnetic frequencies by shielding smart meters and getting cable instead of wireless internet (or at least putting your router outside of the bedroom and living areas). Protect yourself from your cellphone and computer by installing EMF-protecting devices. Make your front door and gate work for you by placing them in the east or north east, or at least according to your ascendant sign. The work you do in the appendix will help to reinforce these tenets as they relate to cultivating purity in the home.

# 11

# In Good Company

*Satsangatve nissangatvam, nissangatve nirmohatvam*
*nirmohatve nishcalatatvam, nischchalatattve samadhi*

"From good company arises detachment from false
attachments; from nonattachment arises freedom
from delusion; out of freedom from illusion there
arises unwavering steadiness, and from unwavering
steadiness arises liberation."

SHANKARACHARYA, FROM *BHAJA GOVINDA*

Following in the footsteps of successful people can be a recipe for your
own success. This is as true in business or sports as it is in spirituality.
Just as a torch lights other torches near it, being in proximity to enlightened souls can kindle your fire, often with little effort on your part.
This is the lazy path to enlightenment, and one of the oldest. Let's take
a look at five ways to practice it.

## FIRST:
## FIND AN ESTIMABLE TEACHER

The first and most obvious way to enlighten yourself through the presence of others is to find a teacher who is higher than you, spiritually
speaking. This would be one who has cleaned and polished their inner
mirror, allowing divine light to reflect in them. Usually this is a guru, a

pastor, or a mentor of some kind. If you're trying to learn a golf swing, you want to hang out with a golf pro to model the good habits you need—from diet and lifestyle to mental attitude to the proper bio-mechanics of your swing.

The problem is that it's hard to find authentic spiritual masters, especially in the digital age where many proclaim truth, but few really live it. One test to know if they are the real deal is the "sandalwood standard." In India they say that real gurus are like sandalwood—the more you scratch, the sweeter they smell. The more you test the guru, the more compassion they emanate. The more you push, the more love you get.

In reality, however, many teachers set themselves up behind institutions and closed doors so it's hard to tell if they're authentic. What happens when you put the guru in tough situations, or pepper them with questions? Do they become angry, frustrated, or impatient? Or do they rise above pettiness and shine, like a star untouched by the darkness around it?

## Guru Stories

*Once, there was a sage who lived on alms. He was so poor that he could hardly scrounge his daily meal. Nonetheless, he was happy, abiding in the state of divine love, seeing God everywhere and in everyone. One day, just as he sat to eat his only meal, a stray dog ambled over, grabbed the food off his plate, and darted away. The man was left with only a small tortilla in his hand. Getting up, he ran after the dog, yelling, "My Lord! My Lord! You forgot the tortilla!"*

*At another time, a yogi sat near the Ganges performing austerities. Nearby he saw a scorpion going into the water. Quickly he rose and ran to the water, picking up the scorpion and depositing him on the bank. No sooner had he done this, the scorpion started again for the river. Again the yogi lifted him from certain death in the water and set him on the shore, a little farther this time. But no sooner had he touched the ground, the scorpion again made for the river.*

*A passerby noticed this and asked the yogi, "Doesn't the scorpion sting you every time you do that?"*

"Yes," the yogi said.

"Then why do you do it? Especially when the scorpion is ungrateful?"

The yogi replied, "It is the scorpion's nature to sting; it is my nature to help."

---

Many spiritual authorities are at best politicians in church robes, and at worst, hypocrites blind to their own hypocrisy—the same as Jesus inveighed when he said, "I assure you and most solemnly say to you that the tax collectors and the prostitutes will get into the kingdom of God before you" (Matthew 21:31 AMP).

How can you tell if your teacher is enlightened? Look to their behavior. Do their deeds reflect their doctrine? Do their lives shine as examples of spiritual truth? In *The Yoga Sutras of Patanjali,* chapter 1, it says that when samadhi (enlightenment) is reached, the seeds of karma are burned. New plants cannot sprout from burnt seeds. Anger, selfishness, and the emotions arising from the delusion of "me" and "mine" are banished.

When you see the face of God you know it to be the face of everyone and you are radically transformed. If someone claims to have seen God but their behavior hasn't changed, their vision is delusion.

"How do you know when someone is enlightened?"

"You see their behavior."

"What should you see?"

"If they still do the same thing, behave the same way with people, they are not changed, only modification is there."

"Modification?"

"The play of the gunas—sattva, rajas, tamas. The enlightened man is beyond the gunas—even sattva—since gunas are attachment: tamas is attached to ignorance and darkness; rajas to activity, and sattva to purity. This is trading one thing for another. I was attached to a worldly thing, now I'm attached to a spiritual thing. When you see the face of God, you cannot be attached to anything, you are radically transformed!"

"What's the difference between sattva and enlightenment?"

"Sattva is the state that brings you to enlightenment. It is the beginning, the door."

A spiritual master in whom the seeds of karma have been burned cannot but love the scorpion—not in spite of its sting, but because of it. They cannot react any other way. If you are blessed with mentors of this caliber, you understand how rare they are. But if you're not, what do you do? Consider spiritual family the next best thing. A community of like-minded people can be invaluable for attaining higher states of awareness.

## SECOND:
## THE IMPORTANCE OF COMMUNITY

As the success of Alcoholics Anonymous and similar organizations attests, having a support group to carry you when you slip, remind you when you forget, and lift you when you want to soar can make the difference between reaching your destination and falling to the wayside. Whether it's your church group, your Buddha bowling buddies, or even your weekly book club meetings, sharing personal stories, spiritual insights, and even grief and suffering with like-minded folks can go a long way to kindling your inner light and keeping it lit forever.

Humans are communal animals and our worst and best instincts are fostered in the group mind. It is good to spend time with like-minded people who work toward a higher good, but be careful that your group does not foster an overly combative (rajasic) or clannish and parochial (tamasic) mind-set.

Working for political change, environmental policy, or even human rights can be noble causes, but they're not necessarily conducive to spiritual insight. If you are an activist, along with your reform work consider grounding yourself in a spiritual community so that you come from the highest place possible when you work for change.

## THIRD:
## THE RELEVANCE OF SCRIPTURE

In the absence of enlightened teachers or a spiritual family you can still encounter the masters of the past using the time machine of books. Reading scripture puts you in touch with the living essence of your spiritual tradition. Dive into the stories and pastimes of gods and saints and some of their essence will rub off on you. You can do this even if you have a spiritual family and a guru—making your torch ever easier to light. Here's a story about the great sage Vyasa, who, though he had compiled the Vedas and authored the longest and perhaps greatest book of all time—the Mahabharata—was still very much human.

*Once, Vyasa was following his son Shuka as he wandered naked through the forest. Shuka had left home to pursue enlightenment and Vyasa, though a highly developed master, like a doting father still yearned for his boy and feared for his safety. Shuka rebuked his dad, telling him that he of all people should know that in Spirit we are all one, and that Spirit would protect him.*

*As they wandered by a group of young girls bathing in a nearby river, Shuka paid no attention and the girls seemed unperturbed by his presence. But when Vyasa came along they immediately grabbed their clothes, sensing that he had not transcended his maleness and lust. He was still subject to the dualities of nature. Vyasa at once realized that, though he had achieved the heights of yogic power and perception, his son had surpassed him in spiritual attainment.*

## FOURTH:
## BABIES EMBODY DIVINE RADIANCE

If you can't find a spiritual group, qualified guru, or books to read, consider spending time with newborn babies. That glow mothers get before and after birth isn't just hormones—it's the aura of enlightenment. Being newly arrived from another world, babies still embody a divine radiance. They are pure, innocent, and light—all qualities of an enlightened being. If you can't find a guru, find a baby, especially if you are also a Pitta mind/body type. That's because innocence melts a Pitta person's heart.

## FIFTH:
## TALK TO ANIMALS

If there are no qualified gurus, groups, books, or babies where you live (Seriously? Where do you live?), or you are too lazy to even read . . . don't despair! There is still a way to stir up good vibes by association, though it is perhaps not as potent as the previous methods. Consider spending time around young animals. Baby goats, kittens, and even foals and calves can melt your heart just like human babies. Use that state of vulnerability and charm and take it with you throughout your day. Volunteer around these animals, or raise them, and translate the compassion you feel to everyone around you!

There are endless ways to raise your vibration: eating an enlightening diet, fasting, performing sacred movement like yoga or dance, meditating, chanting sacred sounds, and deep breathing. But one of the easiest is hanging out with enlightened souls. Try the five methods above and see how they work for you!

# 12

# Live with Purpose

The world's many spiritual traditions all have instructions on how to live. The Bhagavad Gita teaches action without attachment. The Hebrew scriptures and Judaism lay down over six hundred commandments, ten of which are well known. In the Christian scriptures Jesus enjoins us to love our enemies as our friends. And the Buddha proclaims right living and compassion in action.

How can we make sense of all this wisdom when we have bills to pay and families to raise? How do we keep our spiritual priorities clear when there are so many rules, some of them even contradictory? How simple the answer is may surprise you: *do your dharma, and the rules fall into place.* Dharma is your inner path—the reason you were put on this planet. By following it God, love, and prosperity come closer to you. Instead of seeking them out, pursue your dharma and let them find you!

## IT'S EASY TO BE YOU
## WHEN YOU LOVE WHAT YOU DO

Let's take an example of walking the dharmic path. Say you always wanted to be a mechanic, but you got an office job to pay the bills. People call and annoy you every day, making you irritable and anxious. Your manager doesn't help, giving you quotas and rules to follow. What's more, there's a dress code you don't like, and the hours are lousy.

In this scenario trying to follow a spiritual practice becomes ever more difficult because you're already swimming upriver: spiritual rules just add more power to the current.

On the other hand, let's say that you get your mechanic's certification and start working in an auto shop. In this job too you deal with annoying customers, lousy hours, and a boss who is too demanding. The difference is that in the performance of this dharma it is easier to deal with them. It is easier to not only shrug off a complaining customer but to give them a free upgrade to make them happy, knowing that your dharma will bring you more love, support, and opportunity. This is spirituality in action. This is where the golden rule and turning the other cheek become practical in the real world instead of just wishful thinking.

I know it's easy to say, and sometimes life isn't so clear. Sometimes teachers trade in their calculators for cash registers, becoming Merchants to survive. Nonetheless, even as Merchants they will continue to teach because that's their dharma. You cannot change your stripes, and no matter your profession or what relationship you're in, you carry your dharma with you, though some professions are better suited for it than others. Your challenge in any lifetime is to find the best way to express your dharma in the world, even if you're stuck in a less-than-ideal situation. Luckily the ancients gave us a system that makes finding your dharma easy.

In ancient India there are four *varnas*—"colors," tribes, or communities of shared values. There is also a fifth tribe, which is outside the pale of the other four—the explorers and rebels who don't fit into the normal order. Each of us belongs to one of these communities called the five dharma types.

You've probably heard the word *caste* and the social system associated with it. Caste is a degraded, politicized version of the dharma type. In truth, your varna isn't *hereditary* or *hierarchical;* it doesn't depend on the color of your skin, what family you were born into, or your socioeconomic status. It's also nontransferable—you can't "be" someone else just because you want to.* The dharma type is uniquely

*The dharma type is also called *jati*—your "birth nature."

yours; a more current way to describe it is your "operating system"—
the software that runs you regardless of what your hardware looks
like. You were born for a reason; finding that reason is the key to
your happiness. Here is a summary of the dharma associated with
each type.

> Your challenge in any lifetime is to find the best way
> to express your dharma in the world, even if you're stuck
> in a less-than-ideal situation.

## DHARMA SPECIFICS

### Laborer

The Laborer's dharma is to nourish, serve, and create community. The
most practical and "earthy" type, they are handy from a young
age and often not allergic to work. Unlike Educators, who may be
fickle and take many years to grow in wisdom, Laborers come prepared
for life from the get-go. They are the foundation of society.

### Warrior

The Warrior's dharma is to solve problems, and Warriors thrive in
emergencies. If you're not sure if you're a Warrior or another type, consider this: When everything hits the fan and people around you panic,
do you feel calm and centered, like the eye of a hurricane? Do people
naturally turn to you for leadership at these moments? If the answer is
yes, then you are a Warrior type! Warriors do best when there's a problem to be solved and people to be commanded, since Warriors know
how to take control of a situation and thus make natural leaders.

### Merchant

The Merchant's dharma is to make people happy; they often do this by
creating and sharing value. Merchants have a unique talent for entertaining, networking, and finding value where others can't see it. On
the negative side, they often feel empty and try to fill that emptiness
with experiences and "stuff." Their antidote is giving freely to others

what they most want to have; making others happy makes them happy. Hoarding wealth and happiness is a recipe for self-annihilation for the Merchant type.

## *Educator*

The Educator's dharma is to communicate and spread wisdom. They are primarily idea-oriented and have a harder time working solely for money like Merchants can. Their ideals may not meet real-world reality, but that doesn't make them any less valuable. Educators are also natural role models, as they are perceived to be vessels of purity and truth—though they may have trouble living up to that standard due to lust and other vices.

## *Outsider*

The Outsider's dharma is innovation: bringing something new into the world, or blending two or more things that already exist in a way no one ever thought to before, like fusion cuisine or Dr. Martin Luther King's nonviolent movement for social equality. They don't have to reinvent the wheel—more often they bring the wheel to places that don't yet have it. Their dharma is to take technology and wisdom from one culture and introduce it into another.

> You were born for a reason; finding that reason is
> the key to your happiness.

# FIVE PATHS
# TO ENLIGHTENMENT

Each dharma type, with its strengths and weaknesses along with purpose and profession, has an ideal spiritual path. For example, Educators are better at scriptural knowledge than straight devotion, while Laborers have more inherent faith and find solace in a devotional path, regardless of their religion. Whatever your spiritual tradition, here is how your dharma type interfaces with the Divine.

## Laborer

Humans have two thinking centers: the gut and the brain. Laborers are more in touch with their enteric nervous system—their gut—than any other type. As a result their spirituality tends to be faith- and feeling-based. They make the best devotees and also excel at service and evangelism—doing the hard work behind the scenes to keep a church going. That's why they're the foundation of any society or religion. Their weakness is believing that theirs is the only way. If you're a Laborer type, remember that not everyone interfaces with God the way you do, and other paths are just as valid.

Daily devotion in the form of song and music, or rosary or mantra repetition such as the Hare Krishna mantra, and service to the poor are all optimal spiritual disciplines for the Laborer. Sitting at the feet of a guru or master is a favorite pastime. Cooking for and otherwise taking care of such teachers is another way to take advantage of being in good company, which the previous chapter endorses (and which you can reinforce by following the 7 of 11 Method in the appendix).

## Warrior

The Warrior's spiritual gifts are penance and austerity. They would rather complete an intense twenty-day Vipassana retreat (where one rises at 4:00 a.m., eats two small meals, and meditates all day) than simply go to church on Sunday. If there is a spiritual goal to be accomplished, like trekking around Mount Kailash, Warriors are on it. They crave the challenge of an isolated pilgrimage over the hum-drum of daily worship. Being disciplined, however, they can also stay with a routine, especially if it's goal-centered in some way.

## Merchant

The Merchant's is the path of ritual. Rituals like birthday parties and anniversaries underscore the human need for social interaction. Merchants require this interaction more than any other type. As a result, talking to God through prayer and ritual worship is well suited to Merchant types, as is organizing charitable drives, seminars, and spiritual get-togethers. Anything that creates value for their community is a spiritual practice for Merchants.

## Educator

The Educator's role is to interpret ancient wisdom for their time. That means accessing the spiritual languages and scriptures of the past and making them relevant to a diverse audience. Educators are the scholars and priests of the dharma-type family, and they also make good counselors and role models because they are diplomatic, well-rounded, and can see multiple points of view. They serve well as teachers and pastors and can access the Divine through the sacred word. Theirs is the path of wisdom and meditation.

## Outsider

For the Outsider rules (and speed limits) are just suggestions, and it's in their nature to dabble in typically taboo topics. Sacred sexuality, dark arts, astrology (God forbid!), and the occult are par for the course. Even within a standard spiritual tradition they are likely to stretch the bounds of what's acceptable, merging Hindu teachings into a Christian church, or consolidating warring ideologies. The word *occult* simply means "hidden." Finding that which is hidden and bringing it to light is their nature; merging it with what's already known in a way no one has ever thought of before is their special gift. The result is amalgams like shadow yoga, Reggae Kirtan, and the many sacred medleys that renew the spiritual experience.

---

### 5 Elements, 5 Types

In chapter 8 we examined how to harmonize the five elements into your daily life. Here we'll look at how connecting to even one element specific to your dharma type can focus you to achieve your dreams and live your dharma. Each type is associated with an element, as follows:

Earth: Laborer

Water: Merchant

Fire: Warrior

Air: Educator

Space: Outsider

When Laborers integrate the earth element they become rock solid, stable, and anchored to their dharma. They can do this by following the suggestions in chapter 8 and by creating a feeling of security in their lives. That means owning their own home, property, tools, and *stuff.* That comes when they value themselves and their work and charge what they're worth. Laborers should hike often and take trips in nature to stay connected to the earth element.

When Merchants channel the water element, their prosperity flourishes. The most expensive properties lie along the shorelines of the world. Merchants should take extra time to be around water. Water is value, and adding it to their lives—even in the form of staying extra-hydrated all day long—gives Merchants an edge, creating even greater prosperity.

The fire element helps Warriors attain their goals faster. Fire is light and without being able to visualize and see their goals, Warriors stumble. Therefore they must look at their goals daily. Fire is also technology—think electricity and combustion—which lets Warriors complete impossible tasks. Master the tools and technology you need to get ahead. Exposure to the fire element is key for Warriors to achieve their dharma.

Exposure to air inspires Educators with new ideas while refreshing their bodies and rebooting their minds. Biking, riding a motorcycle, horseback riding, sailing, or being out in the fresh breeze is healthy for this type, who tend to stay stuffed up in the laboratory, in front of the computer, or in the classroom too long. Get out and breathe. Your students will thank you!

Having organized space around them helps Outsiders feel calmer. This naturally anxious type gets even more frazzled when the spaces in their bodies and environments are cluttered. Clean the center of your body by fasting once in a while. Clean the center of your home and keep it uncluttered. Then go out and stare at the stars. Your dharma will make itself instantly apparent to you!

# YOGA'S TEN COMMANDMENTS

Just like the Ten Commandments of the Hebrew scriptures, the yogic tradition has its own list of do's and don'ts, called the Five Yamas and Five Niyamas. Here are the Ten Commandments for reference.

---

## THE TEN COMMANDMENTS (EXODUS 20:2–17 NKJV)

**1**   I am the Lord your God, who brought you out of the land of Egypt, out of the house of bondage. You shall have no other gods before Me.

**2**   You shall not make for yourself a carved image, or any likeness of anything that is in heaven above, or that is in the earth beneath, or that is in the water under the earth; you shall not bow down to them nor serve them. For I, the Lord your God, am a jealous God, visiting the iniquity of the fathers on the children to the third and fourth generations of those who hate Me, but showing mercy to thousands, to those who love Me and keep My Commandments.

**3**   You shall not take the name of the Lord your God in vain, for the Lord will not hold him guiltless who takes His name in vain.

**4**   Remember the Sabbath day, to keep it holy. Six days you shall labor and do all your work, but the seventh day is the Sabbath of the Lord your God. In it you shall do no work: you, nor your son, nor your daughter, nor your male servant, nor your female servant, nor your cattle, nor your stranger who is within your gates. For in six days the Lord made the heavens and the earth, the sea, and all that is in them, and rested the seventh day. Therefore the Lord blessed the Sabbath day and hallowed it.

**5**   Honor your father and your mother, that your days may be long upon the land which the Lord your God is giving you.

**6**   You shall not murder.

**7**   You shall not commit adultery.

**8**   You shall not steal.

**9**   You shall not bear false witness against your neighbor.

**10**  You shall not covet your neighbor's house; you shall not covet your neighbor's wife, nor his male servant, nor his female servant, nor his ox, nor his donkey, nor anything that is your neighbor's.

---

By modern moral standards the first five commandments don't really fit the second five: not working on a Saturday hardly seems as weighty as not being a murderer. Taking the Lord's name in vain doesn't stack up with armed robbery in terms of moral flagrancy. For that reason the last five commandments are the ones generally understood and practiced even by non-Jews. They also correspond *exactly* to yoga's Five Yamas. Behind this correspondence is a deeper truth: each Yama and Commandment is also specific to a dharma type. That means that every dharma type has an individual discipline above and beyond the others; by following it they embody the wisdom of *all* the commandments. Here's their correlation.

| Yama | Commandment | Dharma Type |
|---|---|---|
| 1. *Ahimsa:* Nonviolence | "You shall not murder." | Educator |
| 2. *Satyam:* Speaking truth | "You shall not bear false witness." | Warrior |
| 3. *Asteya:* Nonstealing | "You shall not steal." | Merchant |
| 4. *Brahmacharya:* Continence | "You shall not commit adultery." | Laborer |
| 5. *Aparigraha:* Nongrasping | "You shall not covet." | Outsider |

*A yogi was walking down a lonely path when suddenly he was accosted by a thug. "Give me your bag or you'll get a beating!" cried the ruffian.*

*"Lord, please help me, I am your servant!" called the yogi, not wanting to give up his meager possessions.*

*Not waiting for a response, the thug sprang upon the yogi, who bravely resisted, trying to prevent the scoundrel from seizing his stuff. After a brief tussle, the thug overmastered the yogi and ran off with his goods, giving him a sound beating to boot.*

*Then, out of nowhere, the yogi noticed the refulgent Lord standing nearby. "Where were you?" he cried.*

*"I came when I heard your voice," said the Lord, "but when I saw you*

*fighting I couldn't tell who was the yogi and who was the thug."* With that, he disappeared.

The chagrined yogi vowed to never abandon his dharma again and started happily down the path, naked and dispossessed, but blessed to have been in the company of the Divine.

## Spiritual Language

**Educators** are born to transmit wisdom. Their core virtue is *non-violence (ahimsa)*; as a result, their speech should be gentle, empowering, and most of all imbued with wisdom and truth. Your job as an Educator is to leave people with more wisdom and peace in any interaction, preferably without long, drawn out explanations—learn to say more with less.

A special quality of the Educator is the ability to speak the sacred language of their tradition. For Christians it may be Koine Greek, Hebrew, or Aramaic. For students of Vedic wisdom Sanskrit unlocks the secrets of the Vedas. But this talent isn't limited only to spiritual tradition. Scientists, programmers, and musicians all speak a specialized language. It is up to the Educators of the world to teach and interpret those languages. You may not be the greatest guitarist in history, but you may be able to explain music in a way others can understand. You may not be Einstein, but your fluency in math, the lingua franca of most sciences, can translate universal laws into common understanding.

**Warriors** are born to solve problems and feel most at ease during an emergency. Their core virtue is *truth (satyam)*. That means that being gentle is not their first priority—getting directly to the point is. Your goal, Warrior, is to speak truth to power and to leave people with fewer problems than when they met you—or at least with directions on how exactly they can solve those problems. You must learn how to temper your directness as not every situation is an emergency. You can be fewer cutting and critical—it's a matter of learned diplomacy.

**Merchants** are the tale bearers. They can be excitable and over-promise but underdeliver. Their speech is emotional and charged and can get people to do what they want for them. Since your yogic virtue is *non-stealing (asteya),* try to leave people with *more value* than they had before talking with you. That can mean a compliment, a stock tip, or a networking suggestion. When you create value for others your own stock goes up. Cutting people down with your clever tongue only makes you feel worse, so use your gift to create win-win scenarios and to uplift, not to steal.

**Laborers** have the unique ability to nourish others. Their yogic virtue is *continence (brahmacharya),* which means restraining their impulses; saying less and doing more. Body language and a look can say more than a thousand words. In any interaction, try to leave people feeling nourished, understood, and cared for.

**Outsiders** are born to innovate, shock, and rebel. Their yogic virtue is *non-grasping (aparigraha),* which means that at some stage in life, their quest for freedom leads them to free others while sharing their unique expression with the world. Use your speech to create wonder in a way that also promotes progress and liberates people from their problems. You have mystery on your side, but use it to create clarity, not confusion. Telling the truth to yourself and others will set you free.

| DHARMA TYPE | PATH | YAMA | NIYAMA | ELEMENT |
|---|---|---|---|---|
| Laborer | devotion/ service | continence (brahmacharya) | cleanliness | earth |
| Merchant | ritual, charity, karma yoga | nonstealing (asteya) | contentment | water |
| Warrior | karma yoga,* austerity | truth (satyam) | self-control | fire |
| Educator | wisdom/ scripture | nonviolence (ahimsa) | self-study | air |
| Outsider | tantra/tabu/ mystery | nongrasping (aparigraha) | surrender to Divine | space |

*Karma yoga is the discipline of selfless action—working in the world without attachment to the results of your work.

## SHARING YOUR GIFT

Okay, so if you're saying, "I already do that stuff, Simon. It comes naturally to me," then you're exactly right! Doing your dharma isn't something you have to learn from a book—*it's already in you.* Educators are *already* clumsy and smart and lusty and intellectually curious—the point is to encourage some of those qualities and properly channel the others. The point of books like mine is to help you develop your inherent gifts and minimize your shortcomings.

> **Doing your dharma isn't something you have to learn from a book—**
> ***it's already in you.***

Basically, ask yourself, "How would I act on a date?" "How would I behave if I were meeting someone I wanted to impress but also get along with?" When we go out, we try to put our best selves forward. Or, lacking self-confidence, sometimes we make the mistake of trying to be someone else. The problem is, that's hard to do, and in the long run you will feel miserable. Better to be a bad version of *you* than a glammed-up version of another person. Below are some ways to channel your truest and best qualities, whether on a date or in your day-to-day life. Take it from Krishna—it's better to be *bad* at what you do than *good* at what is bad for you!*

### *Educator*
Educators embody a gentle, nonjudgmental quality that makes people open up to them. They should embrace that instead of trying to be tough, gruff, slick, mysterious, or any other qualities not their own. People like Educators because they're smarter than everyone else. They're also naturally unassuming. When they try to become forceful or overbearing they lose the grace nature gives them; the moment they cut themselves off from gentility Educators disconnect from the Divine. Nonviolence, the yogic virtue inherent to their personality,

---

*From the Bhagavad Gita (3:35).

isn't just abstaining from hurt—it means not causing fear in any crea-
ture.* This even applies to plants and animals. Even slamming the
door in the house or yelling can startle and create anxiety. Just because
you can do a thing doesn't mean that you should. Be an ambassador
of divine love and gentle surrender—this is your highest truth. The
moment you brutalize or create fear in others, you pave the way to
disintegration.

## Warrior

For Warriors nonviolence is not the primary virtue. As doctors, for
example, their job is to excise a cancer and fight disease on behalf
of a patient. They cannot do this if they're focused on nonviolence.
What people like about Warriors is their directness, strength, and
confidence. In fact, counter to the Educator, it's the Warrior's dharma
to punish wrongdoers and fight for those who can't defend themselves. That doesn't mean they should be arrogant—quite the opposite. Evolved Warriors carry a quiet confidence that's palpable. On a
date it makes them appear strong without having to brag about themselves. In fact the Warrior's virtue is speaking truth. Truth means telling a patient they are sick and preparing them for the battle to come.
Truth means saying you will be somewhere and being there exactly
on time.

Truth is also the ability to control your breath and so too your
mind. Speech aligns *intention* with *breath*. Learning to control your
breath with measured speaking, deep breathing, and aerobic exercise is
vital for your spiritual evolution. Aligning your speech with your values
is also one of the highest aspects of this commandment. When no one
dares rise up against tyranny it is the Warrior's duty to speak up and tell
it like it is. The other dharma types will emulate you, because speaking
your truth gives everyone a voice.

---

*Being almost six foot four, I have learned not to sneak up on or walk in ways that
startle people, especially at night. Just because I *can* do it doesn't mean that it's what's
best for my evolution.

## *Merchant*

For Merchants the primary virtue is giving energy and value to others and not taking more than is your due. The opposite of stealing is charity—giving what you have in plenty to those who don't. If you're poor that could simply mean a smile and a compliment, but usually Merchants have "stuff" to give away, and doing so is their path to redemption.

*Asteya* also means not stealing another's thunder. Showing up others with superior wit or skill only makes you feel good in the short term. Do the opposite—make people feel big. Make them laugh and pump them with good energy and you will win both worldly and spiritual success.

## *Laborer*

The Laborer's virtue is continence. If you're a Laborer you should practice abstinence from sex when you're young and fidelity in your marriage. Promiscuity creates problems for Laborers because it takes them away from their core ethic, which is family, community, and devotion. That doesn't mean that you can't have sex before marriage—it simply means that containing sexual energy will make you healthier, stronger, sexier, and give you more spiritual insight.

Because the tongue is a secondary "sex organ," this also means controlling your appetites for food as well as restraining your speech. You may want to lash out, but speaking truth to power is the Warrior's virtue. Better to contain your ire and transform it into love and devotion. This process of withdrawing your energy inward is like the black hole at the center of our galaxy. By the power of its gravity it contains all explosive energy and light. As a result it becomes the most irresistible force around which all other stars and planets revolve. Your dharma, Laborer, is the power of continence to withdraw your sense energy inward so you become a bright ball of love within, even though only those who know you well can see that light.

## *Outsider*

The Outsider's virtue is being free and nongrasping. The moment you grasp for something you lose your freedom, and your freedom is what people admire about you. Outsiders are extremely adaptable and can blend, taking on different identities, but at some point in their lives Outsiders must say, "Who am I really, and what is my gift?" When they do that they stop grasping at other identities and create their own unique expression. This unique expression is the key to their fulfillment. Do not covet your neighbor's house with the picket fence. If you had it you'd grow bored within a week and miserable within a month. Cherish your unique freedom to be who you want to be and stop grasping for what you're not.

## YOUR PATH, YOUR DHARMA

In astrology the tenth house represents your "career." It also indicates fame, success, and fortune. The sixth house on the other hand is your "job," but also disease, debt, and discord. It's the primary house of "divorce" as well. Astrology reflects reality: work at a "job" for too long and you will lose the respect of your friends, your partner, and even yourself. Find your career and work at it and you will find success, no matter how humble that career may be. We all have to work at "jobs," (sixth house) especially when we're young or in dire economic times. It takes an extraordinary individual, despite those hardships, to find time for their true calling in order to express their dharma in the world (tenth house).

It's hard to be true when you hate what you do. When you fail to align with your dharma completely you feel like a fraud—like an actor playing a part you were not really meant for. Arnold Schwarzenegger was convincing as the Terminator, but not as Kindergarten Cop. In the same way, knowing your dharma type can help you find the part you're best suited for—the role for which you'll be remembered. The appendix that follows will show you how to accrue points for doing your dharma or performing the spiritual practice for your dharma type. This method is the hardest to judge, but it's also the most important.

*Some years ago I asked my mentor, "Sir, you've shown me many paths to enlightenment, but they're all so hard . . . and I'm so lazy. What's the **best thing** a person can do to bring blessing into their life?"*

*He flashed a smile and without hesitating replied: "Feed people. It is the best spiritual practice."*

It took years to sink in, but he was right. If, disregarding everything else in this book, you go out of your way to feed people—especially the hungriest and the neediest—without attachment or pride, you will likely accrue spiritual, emotional, and physical benefits as if you had dedicatedly performed the 7 of 11 Method. What's more, do it regularly and on an auspicious day, and you stand to gain even more. What's an auspicious day? The day ruled by the sixth pada lord in your Vedic horoscope is one. For other options (and for a full explanation of what that means), consult your local friendly astrologer!

# Let Your Light Shine

Even one method practiced with devotion and one-pointed focus will take you to your goal. Of all these, the best is doing your dharma. Without dharma there is no guarantee that the techniques in this book will work. Why did we wait until chapter 12 to bring it up? Because in Vedic scriptures the most crucial elements are both at the beginning and the end. In the early pages of this book we began with the idea that enlightenment is available to everyone. It is your born right and humanity's ultimate goal. Here we end with the simplest and perhaps most important method to achieve enlightenment: following your dharma.

> **Even one method practiced with devotion
> and one-pointed focus will take you to the goal.
> Of all these, the best is doing your dharma.**

Imagine that you have a good ship with a knowledgeable captain and a strong motor. But without accurate maps the journey will be uncertain, even perilous. That is because, without a guiding principle, even a pure life is less than fulfilling. Purity (sattva) alone is nothing without direction (dharma).

In fact it's possible to have *too much* purity. When some students begin to experience harmony in their bodies and minds they can become self-righteous and even insufferable. Purity is sattva, and in the act of obtaining it sometimes you want others to experience it too, leading you to proselytize, pounding your "sattva" bible so to speak, to people who don't want to hear it. The antidote is simple: let your sattva speak for itself.

Instead of converting others, act like a candle kindling other candles by the proximity of its flame. Sattva converts by touching those who are ready to catch fire. Those who are wet will never light but turn to smoke instead. Avoid this smoke and confusion and abide in your being. Your actions, presence, and purity will attract those who are ready.

The danger of ungrounded sattva is that one may also get lost in spiritual pride. You may get to a point of purity in your practice that makes you believe you've made it and that you're so much better than others around you. This is a lie. Remember, everyone has the spark of spirit, though it may be hidden. Remember also that there are others whose mirror shines far more brightly than yours. In martial arts circles truly advanced practitioners tend to be humble because they know there is always another expert better than they are. In spiritual circles it is the same. There are always masters who are light-years ahead of you. Remember that and stay humble. Humility invites grace, and grace catapults you to enlightenment beyond your expectations!

# Daily Planner—The 7 of 11 Dharma Method

You don't need to spend all day in the lotus position or shell out thousands of dollars on seminars and guru initiations to connect to the Divine. Whether you're just dipping your toes into spiritual waters or if you've been immersed in them for years, the 7 of 11 Method will help you find your inner bliss while tracking your progress as it grows.

Give yourself a point for each practice you try today and keep a journal of your progress. Shoot for seven points daily, no matter how you get there. You don't have to repeat the same things. Life is flexible, and your spiritual life should be flexible too. The Dharma Method is designed to live with you, to change and adapt to your day-to-day life. With more than twenty ways to make points, you can easily find seven in your day no matter where you are or what you're doing.

If you're having your menses you may not want to do breathwork or exercise. If you're on a trip you may not have access to a sacred space. The 7 of 11 Method gives you options and alternatives, choices, and workarounds to keep you on the path to enlightenment without derailing your schedule.

> You don't have to do the same things every day. Life is flexible, and your spiritual life should be flexible too.

## SYNERGY

When you consistently practice the Dharma Method, you'll create a synergy that makes each of the techniques easier than if you were just doing them alone. For example, it's easier to pull off getting up with the dawn when you're also fasting; it's easier to fast when you're passionately following your dharma; it's easier to do your dharma when you meditate and invite Spirit into your life; it's easier to meditate when you do sacred movement, and so forth. When you add in seven or more enlightening techniques you get a result that is more than the sum of its parts.

Here are the eleven techniques summarized, by chapter. After the list, you'll find fun ways to customize them into a challenging game.

### Rise and Shine (chapter 2)
- Give yourself a point for getting up at or before sunrise.
- Give yourself an additional point for greeting the sun for at least fifteen minutes with sun gazing, exposure, or yoga.
- Give yourself two points for being up during the Brahma muhurta, the hour of spirit.
- Give yourself a point for honoring the sunset with fifteen to forty-five minutes of stillness. (This is also the A.M. to P.M. practice from chapter 4.)

### Breathe for Life (chapter 3)
- Give yourself a point for fifteen to forty-five minutes of deep breathing today.

### The Space Within (chapter 4)
- Give yourself a point for each time you practiced active or passive meditation (A.M. or P.M.) fifteen to forty-five minutes today. Remember that both are necessary, and they're especially effective during auspicious times like sunrise, sunset, or the Brahma muhurta.

### Sacred Food (chapter 5)
- Cleaning up your diet will directly improve your spiritual awareness. Give yourself a point for eating primarily *enlightening* food. This includes pure dairy, fresh fruit and vegetables, and grains

and legumes. This excludes most meat and fish, heavily fried or spiced ingredients, and fermented foods.

- Give yourself a point for adding ritual to at least two meals today. Saying grace, lighting a candle, or cooking from scratch adds deliberate awareness to mealtime, leading to a pure body and mind.
- Give yourself a point for blessing your food by offering it on your altar to the Divine.
- If you honored your ancestors or performed a fire ceremony today, give yourself a point.

## Sacred Sound (chapter 6)

- Sacred sound practice like mantra or prayer is another form of active meditation (A.M.). Give yourself a point if you did fifteen minutes or more of mantra, prayer, or manifestation practice—but this point only counts once—you don't get a point for active meditation *and* for sacred sound since it's the same thing . . . (no cheating!).
- Give yourself a point if you did the quiet So Hum meditation apart from the above practices. Also, if you chanted while you cooked for at least thirty minutes or performed other household duties, give yourself a point. (Since So Hum breathing is meditation, do not give yourself an extra point for passive meditation.)

## Sacred Movement (chapter 7)

- Give yourself another point if you got "sacred & sweaty" today by hiking, dancing, or running with reverence while focused on your breath. Exercise followed by shavasana—Corpse pose—also becomes sacred movement. Give yourself another point if you followed your exercise today with this form of passive meditation. A good yoga class followed by shavasana, for example, gets 2 points.

## Inside Out (chapter 8)

Give yourself a point if you can check off at least four of the five elements below.

- **Earth:** You went for a hike, or walked barefoot on the sand, grass, or bare earth long enough to let the stress drain from your body.

You slept on a mat on the floor or sat on the ground for extended periods. Rolling on the ground (even in the snow), playing in the mud (or getting a mud treatment), or working with bricks and clay also count.

- **Water:** You took a dip in a lake, ocean, or stream; you swam laps in the pool, took a cold shower (at least thirty seconds), or rolled around in the snow (there's the snow again).

- **Fire:** You lit a fire with your bare hands (not by clicking a switch). You exposed at least a third of your body to the sun for at least fifteen minutes. You greeted the morning sun with reverence. Early morning sun gazing for a few seconds also counts, as does candle gazing.

- **Air:** You took a bike ride, rode a horse, or sailed a boat (this counts for water too!). You hiked to the top of a hill and felt the breeze (this counts as earth!). You practiced deep breathing as described in chapter 3. You rode your convertible or motorcycle down an unpopulated street or a fresh-air highway.

- **Space:** You spent time looking at the sky—day or night. You spent time alone in nature—even if for fifteen minutes. This includes walking around a golf course, a park, or even a parking lot. You spent time in an isolation or flotation chamber.

- Some of these, like contemplating the rising sun, count as a full point in and of themselves. But if you collectively honored four out of the five elements above, give yourself an additional point. Nature's elements are easy to combine with other activities, like breathing or sacred movement (chapters 3 and 7). By getting up at dawn (1 point) and contemplating the sun (1 point), then doing your breath exercises (1 point) and meditation (1 point) you are already well on your way to completing the seven items on your daily checklist.

## Life in the "Fast" Lane (chapter 9)

Creating space by fasting is the oldest and most-effective spiritual practice in the world. There are several ways to incorporate fasting into your lifestyle.

- Intermittent fasting: do not eat for at least twelve hours between dinner the night before and breakfast the day of. Give yourself 1 point for this practice every day you do it.
- High-level intermittent fasting: eat all your food for the day within a progressively shorter window—moving from a 12-hour window per day (point 1 above), to 8 hours, 4 hours, and, ultimately you may be able to reduce your feeding time to 2 hours per day. Give yourself 2 points for an 8-hour window, 3 points for a 4-hour window, and 4 points for a 2-hour window.
- Full-day 24-hour fast: do not eat between dinner the night before and dinner the day of the fast. Give yourself 5 points for a full day fast.
- Morning to morning fast: 36 hours from dinner on day 1 to breakfast on day 3. Give yourself 5 points for the full day you fast and 2 points for the next day you break the fast. Try to do a 24 or 36 hour fast once a week, or at least once per month—it's the most foundational spiritual practice there is. Besides, you get a lot of points for it . . . good for lazies like me.
- Coffee, licorice, or dashamula enema, or all together with sesame oil and rock salt, is another fantastic way to create space in the body. Give yourself a point if you do this practice today!

## Home Sweet Home (chapter 10)

- Give yourself a point if you cleaned or decluttered your house today and kept it that way, while keeping EMF devices away from your person, and spent time and opened up the light in the northeast direction in your home.
- Or give yourself a point for going without any TV or screen time for the day.

## In Good Company (chapter 11)

- Give yourself a point if you hung around like-minded, enlightened folks today, or held a baby for thirty minutes, or volunteered to spend time with small animals, or read scripture for at least an hour.
- Give yourself an extra point or more if you were lucky enough to spend time with a real spiritual master.

**Live with Purpose (chapter 12)**

- Give yourself a point for doing your dharma today. This method is the hardest to judge, but it's also the most important. There is a sense you get when you are in the flow of your dharma. Reward yourself when you feel it.

If you're adventurous, you can try the following fun practices.

## ◇ LUCKY RANDOM 7

Write out the eleven practices (as described in chapters 2 through 12) on note cards. Shuffle the deck and pick seven out of the eleven cards at random, and do those practices for the day. Whatever cards fall your way, try to get seven points using those methods.

## ◇ SUPER ADVANCED LUCKY RANDOM 5

If you're even more adventurous, try picking only four or five cards. This way, you're forced to make the most of these practices to get to seven points. For example, you might draw: Sacred Food, Rise and Shine, Breathe for Life, and Life in the "Fast" Lane.

Out of these you might give yourself points for blessing your food (1 point), eating only enlightening food (1 point), intermittent fasting for twenty hours (3 points), getting up with the dawn and greeting the sun (2 points). This way, your 7 points come from only four disciplines. Practice this as you become more advanced. Eventually, enlightenment may come from only one of these. When done right, deeply and without distraction, even one of the eleven methods can take you to nirvana.

Ramakrishna, a nineteenth-century saint, achieved samadhi watching cranes flying in the sky. Being in nature, fasting, or meditating—any of the methods by themselves can bring you to a place of bliss. But to get there practice all of them at different times to see what fits for you.

> When done right, deeply and without distraction, even one of the eleven methods can take you to nirvana.

# Notes

## CHAPTER 2.
## RISE AND SHINE

1. Sarah DiGiulio, "The Training Secret Novak Djokovic and 9 Other Pro Athletes Swear By," *Huffington Post,* September 9, 2016, www.huffington post.com/entry/djokovic-training-secrets_us_57c88f2fe4b0e60d31de3dc0?

## CHAPTER 3.
## BREATHE FOR LIFE

1. "Science: The Science behind the Wim Hof Method," Wim Hof Method, accessed February 12, 2018, www.wimhofmethod.com/pages/science.
2. Matthijs Kox et al., "Voluntary Activation of the Sympathetic Nervous System and Attenuation of the Innate Immune Response in Humans," *Proceedings of the National Academy for Sciences* 111, no. 20 (May 20, 2014): 7379–384, www.ncbi.nlm.nih.gov/pmc/articles/PMC4034215.
3. "Yogic Breathing Helps Fight Major Depression, Penn Study Shows," *Penn Medicine News,* November 22, 2016, www.pennmedicine.org/news /news-releases/2016/november/yogic-breathing-helps-fight-ma.
4. Vasant Lad, *Pranayama for Self-Healing,* DVD (Albuquerque, N. Mex.: The Ayurvedic Press, 2010).
5. Paul E. Greenberg, "The Growing Economic Burden of Depression in the U.S.," *Scientific American,* February 25, 2015, https://blogs.scientificamerican.com /mind-guest-blog/the-growing-economic-burden-of-depression-in-the-u-s.

## CHAPTER 4. THE SPACE WITHIN

1. "Ram Dass on Giving Maharajji LSD," www.maharajji.com/Satsang-Video
/ram-dass-on-giving-maharaji-lsd.html. See also Ram Dass, *Be Here Now*
(New York: Three Rivers Press, 1971).

## CHAPTER 5. SACRED FOOD

1. Redzo Mujcic and Andrew J. Oswald, "Evolution of Well-Being and
Happiness after Increases in Consumption of Fruit and Vegetables," *American
Journal of Public Health,* August 2016, http://ajph.aphapublications
.org/doi/10.2105/AJPH.2016.303260.

2. Tamlin S. Conner et al., "Let Them Eat Fruit! The Effect of Fruit and
Vegetable Consumption on Psychological Well-Being in Young Adults: A
Randomized Controlled Trial," PLOS, February 3, 2017, http://journals
.plos.org/plosone/article?id=10.1371/journal.pone.0171206.

3. Usha Lad and Vasant Lad, *Ayurvedic Cooking for Self-Healing* (Albuquerque,
N. Mex.: Ayurvedic Press, 1997).

4. Kathleen D. Vohs et al., "Rituals Enhance Consumption," July 17, 2013,
*Psychological Science,* 24 (9): 1714–21, http://journals.sagepub.com/doi/abs
/10.1177/0956797613478949?journalCode=pssa; Catherine Saint Louis,
"Rituals Make Our Food More Flavorful," August 9, 2013, *The New York
Times,* https://well.blogs.nytimes.com/2013/08/09/rituals-make-our-food
-more-flavorful. Also see my book *Sex, Love, and Dharma* for more on this
topic.

5. Cody C. Delistrati, "The Importance of Eating Togther," July 18, 2014,
*The Atlantic,* https://www.theatlantic.com/health/archive/2014/07
/the-importance-of-eating-together/374256. See also Timi Gustafson,
"Eating Together as a Family Has Multiple Benefits," November 20, 2012,
*Huffington Post,* https://www.huffingtonpost.com/timi-gustafson/family
-dinner_b_1898387.html.

## CHAPTER 6. SACRED SOUND

1. For more information on this technique, which was taught to me by Vasant
Lad, please refer to his book *Secrets of the Pulse* (Albuquerque, N. Mex.:
Ayurvedic Press, 2006). You can also visit www.ayurveda.com for more
information on lectures and courses by Vasant Lad.

## CHAPTER 8.
## INSIDE OUT

1. Mark J Nieuwenhuijsen et al., "Positive Health Effects of the Natural Outdoor Environment in Typical Populations in Different Regions in Europe (PHENOTYPE): A Study Programme Protocol," April 16, 2014, http://bmjopen.bmj.com/content/4/4/e004951.full.


## CHAPTER 9.
## LIFE IN THE "FAST" LANE

1. *Eat Less, Live Longer* from the episode *Never Say Die,* Scientific American Frontiers, season 10 episode 3, posted April 11, 2011, accessed March 8, 2018, www.youtube.com/watch?v=9jvqNG1g62Y&t=234s.
2. Joseph Mercola, "How to Slim Your Waistline without Depriving Yourself," May 8, 2011, http://articles.mercola.com/sites/articles/archive/2011/05/08 /ori-hofmekler-on-undereating-and-exercise.aspx.
3. Catherine R. Marinac et al., "Prolonged Nightly Fasting and Breast Cancer Diagnosis," *JAMA,* August 2016, https://jamanetwork.com/journals /jamaoncology/fullarticle/2506710.
4. Clare Wilson, "Hungry Stomach Hormone Promotes Growth of New Brain Cells," *NewScientist,* April 25, 2017, https://www.newscientist.com /article/2128695-hungry-stomach-hormone-promotes-growth-of-new-brain -cells.
5. Locke Hughes, "How Does Too Much Sugar Affect Your Body?" *WebMD,* March 23, 2017, https://www.webmd.com/diet/features/how-sugar-affects -your-body.
6. Hesham R. Omar et al., "Licorice Abuse: Time to Send a Warning Message," *Therapeutic Advances in Endocrinology and Metabolism* 3, no. 4 (August 2012): 125–38, www.ncbi.nlm.nih.gov/pmc/articles/PMC3498851 /#bibr64-2042018812454322.
7. M. Bernardi et al., "Effects of Prolonged Ingestion of Graded Doses of Licorice by Healthy Volunteers," *Life Science* 55, no. 11 (1994): 863–72, accessed March 8, 2018, www.ncbi.nlm.nih.gov/pubmed/8072387.


## CHAPTER 10. HOME SWEET HOME

1. For information on devices to protect your home, cell phone, and computer from harmful EMR, visit www.defendershield.com or www.hedronlifesource.com.

Special ear buds that do not contain electronics in the earpiece are made by Defendershield and other companies.

2. For full studies and reports, visit "Bioinitiative 2012 A Rationale for Biologically-Based Exposure Standards for Low-Intensity Electromagnetic Radiation," accessed March 15, 2018, www.bioinitiative.org.

# Index

# BOOKS OF RELATED INTEREST

**The Five Dharma Types**
Vedic Wisdom for Discovering Your Purpose and Destiny
*by Simon Chokoisky*

**Sex, Love, and Dharma**
Ancient Wisdom for Modern Relationships
*by Simon Chokoisky*

**Gambler's Dharma**
Sports Betting with Vedic Astrology
*by Simon Chokoisky*

**Being Present**
Cultivate a Peaceful Mind through Spiritual Practice
*by Darren Cockburn*

**Effortless Living**
Wu-Wei and the Spontaneous State of Natural Harmony
by Jason Gregory
*Foreword by Damo Mitchell*

**Fasting the Mind**
Spiritual Exercises for Psychic Detox
*by Jason Gregory*

**The Humming Effect**
Sound Healing for Health and Happiness
*by Jonathan Goldman and Andi Goldman*
*Foreword by John Beaulieu, N.D., Ph.D.*

**Breathing through the Whole Body**
The Buddha's Instructions on Integrating Mind, Body, and Breath
*by Will Johnson*

INNER TRADITIONS • BEAR & COMPANY
P.O. Box 388
Rochester, VT 05767
1-800-246-8648
www.InnerTraditions.com

Or contact your local bookseller